PROSPECTS FOR ADJUSTMENT

PROSPECTS FOR ADJUSTMENT

In Argentina, Brazil, and Mexico

Responding to the Debt Crisis

Edited by
John Williamson

INSTITUTE FOR INTERNATIONAL ECONOMICS
WASHINGTON, DC
June 1983
Distributed by MIT Press/Cambridge, London, Tokyo

Dr. John Williamson is a Senior Fellow at the Institute for International Economics. He was formerly Professor of Economics at leading universities in Brazil, England, and the United States, Consultant to H.M. Treasury, and Advisor to the International Monetary Fund.

INSTITUTE FOR INTERNATIONAL ECONOMICS
C. Fred Bergsten, *Director*
Kathleen A. Lynch, *Director of Publications*
Rosanne Gleason, *Publications Assistant*

The Institute for International Economics was created, and is principally funded, by The German Marshall Fund of the United States.

Library of Congress Catalog Card Number 83-81496
ISBN 0-88132-016-1
Distributed by MIT Press/Cambridge, London, Tokyo
ISBN 0-262-59019-0

Contents

Preface, *C. Fred Bergsten* *page vii*

Introduction, *Miguel A. Kiguel* and *John Williamson* *page 1*

1. Progress and Prospects for the Adjustment Program in Argentina, *José Maria Dagnino Pastore* *page 7*

   Discussion, *Miguel A. Kiguel* *page 27*

2. The IMF and the Prospects for Adjustment in Brazil, *Edmar L. Bacha* *page 31*

   Discussion, *Rudiger Dornbusch* *page 43*

3. The Exchange Crisis and Adjustment Program in Mexico, *Ariel Buira* *page 51*

   Discussion, *William R. Cline* *page 61*

Preface

The debt problem represents a major threat to the stability of the world financial system, to recovery from the recession of the early 1980s and to the prospects of the numerous debtor countries. The external debt of the developing and East European countries exceeds $700 billion, and credits to these countries approximate 300 percent of the capital of the nine largest US banks.

The debt issue has thus been a major focus of the activities of the Institute for International Economics. In August 1982 and May 1983, we published studies by John Williamson on the role of the International Monetary Fund in lending to debtor countries (and others) and helping devise adjustment programs for them. In July and September 1983, we will publish comprehensive studies by William R. Cline on the overall problem and what can be done about it. In addition, we have held several discussion meetings to consider various aspects of the issue.

At the moment, however, one of the most critical developments concerning international debt is the course of the stabilization efforts undertaken by the three largest borrowing countries: Argentina, Brazil, and Mexico. Together, they account for over one-third of the outstanding debt. Successful completion of their current programs would go far toward resolving the problem in a stable way, whereas failure of one or more of them could renew intense pressure on both the world economy and financial system.

The Institute thus decided to hold a conference on May 12 to review the outlook for the "ABM countries," and to draw implications for global arrangements. The discussions were based on papers prepared by outstanding economists from each country, and expert discussion on them. In view of the importance and timeliness of the issue, we here publish those papers and comments in an effort to advance understanding of the outlook for the three major debtors and hence for resolution of the international debt problem.

The Institute for International Economics is a private nonprofit research institution for the study and discussion of international economic policy. Its purpose is to analyze important issues in that area and to develop and communicate practical new approaches for dealing with them. Unlike most of its publications, this one does not aim to develop original proposals for dealing with problems over the medium term but rather seeks to convey to a wider audience the results of an Institute conference with important implications for a current policy issue.

The Institute was created in November 1981 through a generous commitment of funds from the German Marshall Fund of the United States. Financial support has also been received from other private foundations and corporations. The Institute is completely nonpartisan.

The Board of Directors bears overall responsibility for the Institute and gives general guidance and approval to its research program—including identification of topics that are likely to become important to international economic policymakers over the medium run (generally, one to three years) and which should be addressed by the Institute. The Director of the Institute, working closely with the staff and outside Advisory Committee, is responsible for the development of particular projects.

The Institute hopes that its studies and other activities will contribute to building a stronger foundation for international economic policy around the world. Comments as to how it can best do so are invited from readers of these publications.

C. Fred Bergsten
Director

Introduction

Miguel A. Kiguel and John Williamson

The "debt crisis" hit the headlines in mid-1982, when Mexico found itself unable to maintain debt-service payments. The difficulties quickly spread to other countries, especially in Latin America, and soon both Argentina and Brazil—the other two largest debtor developing countries—faced similar emergencies. Defaults or prolonged moratoria by major debtors could have threatened the stability of the international banking system and provoked a collapse of economic activity in debtor countries cut off from a continued flow of imports.

The big three Latin American debtors and a number of smaller countries responded to this situation by seeking short-term bridging loans, followed by medium-term "rescue packages." These packages were negotiated with the International Monetary Fund (IMF). The first task was to design an agreed adjustment program intended to produce a major improvement in the current account of the balance of payments. In each case this included—of necessity, in view of the urgency of the task—a sharp move toward domestic austerity. Second, the Fund gave its formal approval to the program and put up a significant sum of money to help finance the deficit that will inevitably persist until the agreed adjustment programs have time to take full effect. So much is standard Fund practice: the country negotiates an adjustment program that the

Dr. Kiguel is a research associate at the Institute for International Economics; Dr. Williamson, a senior fellow.

Fund deems adequate to the task, and in return the Fund lends money to enable adjustment to be less precipitous than would otherwise be necessary.[1] A third element of the package was more novel: it involved the Fund's organizing the commercial banks to reschedule maturing debts and to lend a significant sum of "new money."

The stand-by agreements signed with the IMF by Argentina, Brazil, and Mexico between December 1982 and February 1983 marked the end of the first stage of the debt crisis. Whether there is a second stage depends on whether the adjustment programs agreed by the big debtors lead to the results expected, or whether those programs break down. In view of the critical importance of this issue, the Institute for International Economics held a conference on May 12, 1983, to assess the progress of, and the outlook for, those adjustment programs. The speakers were asked to address the following questions:

- Were the programs adopted appropriate to the needs of the situation, given the scale of the financial resources available and the state of the world economy?
- How severe are the import reductions in prospect, and what are the implications both for the countries in question and for the world economy?
- Are the programs on course, or is there a serious risk of failure to meet the agreed targets? What would be the consequences of such failure for the countries and for the world?

With regard to the first question, there was far less criticism of Argentina's and Mexico's adjustment programs than of the Brazilian program. Professor José Maria Dagnino Pastore, who was finance minister for a period during 1982, argued that the worst part of the crisis in Argentina was already past. The additional money that will be needed to sustain the program in Argentina appears fairly modest and well within the capacity of the international financial system to provide. The Fund showed more flexibility than it used to in accepting that an adjustment program should be varied to match each country's particular circumstances, and the balance of payments appears to be developing as hoped.

Dr. Ariel Buira, Deputy Director of the Banco de Mexico, also gave a fairly optimistic picture of the program that had been adopted by Mexico. While Mexico's cutback in growth had to be a good deal more

[1] See John Williamson, ed., *IMF Conditionality* (Washington: Institute for International Economics, 1983), especially chapters 4 and 24 and the country studies in Part III.

severe than was necessary in Argentina, partly because previous growth rates had been so much more rapid, a program based on a large reduction in the budget deficit has been accepted as appropriate and necessary and the outlook is for sufficient external finance to make the agreed program viable.

In contrast, Professor Edmar L. Bacha of the Pontifícia Universidade Católica do Rio de Janeiro argued that the Brazilian program was deficient in two crucial ways. First, the financial resources appear inadequate to permit the agreed program to be implemented even if the balance of payments develops as hoped and even if Brazil were able to accomplish everything that it had promised. This problem arises in part because many smaller banks have withdrawn deposits with Brazilian banks in the interbank market. Second, the performance criteria regarding the size of the public sector deficit and the pace of monetary expansion appear totally unrealistic[2] in the light of the acceleration in the rate of inflation that has already taken place. That acceleration in the rate of inflation was a consequence of the need to undertake a maxi-devaluation of the cruzeiro so as to improve the prospects for achieving the target for the current account of the balance of payments. Bacha argued that the Fund should frame performance criteria in terms of real variables which are relevant to the achievement of the balance of payments objectives rather than in terms of nominal variables, whose values should be adjusted in accordance with the evolution of events, especially when those nominal targets apply to internal goals.

All three countries have been obliged to undertake a major compression in their import volume, but this has been sharpest in Mexico and perhaps most painful in Brazil. Argentina appears to have accepted its reduction in import volume with relatively little pain, presumably because the reduction in volume was smaller than in the other two cases. In the case of Mexico, imports in the first quarter of 1983 were running at a third the level a year earlier. Such a drastic compression was possible only because the preceding boom had been extreme and resulted in much excess demand spilling over into imports, but even so the import decline has been painful and has dictated a sharp drop in industrial activity as a result of a shortage of imported inputs. (Industrial production in the first quarter of 1983 was 11 percent below its level a year earlier.)

---

[2] This assessment was subsequently confirmed by the suspension of disbursements under the Brazilian program, pending renegotiation, on May 24.

Imports in Brazil are targeted to decline by 17.5 percent in volume when they were already repressed to a point which had imposed near zero growth[3] on the normally dynamic Brazilian economy for the two preceding years. In consequence Brazil is facing a third straight year of declining per capita income and cannot expect to regain the income level of 1980 until 1987.

So far as the third question is concerned, all three countries appear to be making surprisingly good progress toward achieving the balance of payments component of their targets. Even in Brazil, Bacha was optimistic about the probability of reaching something close to the projected $6 billion trade surplus this year—and without including what he termed the "creative accounting" that aided the rather spectacular trade surpluses posted for March and April. In terms of the internal targets, however, only in Mexico do there seem to be reasonable grounds for confidence that the Fund's performance criteria will be fulfilled. In Brazil the targets expressed in nominal magnitudes are already quite unrealistic, as noted above. Argentina may face similar difficulties by the end of the year, if the high rate of inflation continues.

The Fund is starting to renegotiate the performance criteria that it had previously agreed with Brazil. It is going to need to provide more leeway for monetary growth and the fiscal deficit. Given the sacrifices that Brazil has already made and the good progress that has been achieved toward securing the balance of payments target, it would be foolish—and dangerous for the world economy—not to give Brazil some extra leeway to accommodate the acceleration in the rate of inflation.[4] But if Brazil's violation of its performance criteria is condoned, the question arises as to whether there is much point in imposing such conditions in the first place. Perhaps Fund performance criteria should be recast to focus on progress toward achieving the payments objective, with internal policies relevant only in assessing whether a failure to achieve the external objective had been caused by exogenous developments or by failure to implement agreed policies. Or perhaps "contingent conditions," providing for automatic adaptation of performance criteria in the light of changes in circumstances (such as the rate of inflation), as recommended in section 5 of *The Lending Policies of the International*

[3] −2 percent in 1981 and +1.4 percent in 1982.

[4] One may hope for Brazilian action to modify the indexation formulae and reduce subsidies to agricultural credit, but even these actions would be unlikely to restore the realism of the existing targets.

Monetary Fund,[5] could have avoided the present interruption of the Brazilian program and its inherent risks. Another possibility, advocated in Bacha's paper, would be to couch the internal targets in real terms.

A second adjustment to the Brazilian program may prove even more difficult. *Someone* is going to have to provide substantial additional funds—either in the form of "new money" or of a major rescheduling—if even more drastic Brazilian austerity measures are to be avoided. The debt crisis is clearly not yet over.

[5] John Williamson, *The Lending Policies of the International Monetary Fund*, POLICY ANALYSES IN INTERNATIONAL ECONOMICS, no. 1 (Washington: Institute for International Economics, August 1982).

1 *Progress and Prospects for the Adjustment Program in Argentina*

José Maria Dagnino Pastore

To understand Argentina's economic problems, the consequences of its anti-inflationary policy experiment from December 1978 to March 1981 under Minister of Economy Martinez de Hoz must be briefly analyzed. The experiment's design and development have been extensively described and analyzed elsewhere.[1] As other studies have emphasized, a central cause of the external imbalance by early 1981 was the severe overvaluation caused by the unsuccessful attempt to use a preannounced exchange rate as an anti-inflationary device. When the experiment ended, Argentina was left with a number of economic problems:

- a foreign debt of $29.6 billion (equivalent to 3.7 years of exports), 51 percent of it due in the next 12 months
- a current account deficit running at $2.1 billion a quarter and $6.1 billion over the previous year, with remittances for interest and profits amounting to $0.7 and $2.2 billion, respectively
- declining fiscal revenues, which covered only 56 percent of expenditures in the previous quarter

---

Dr. Pastore, formerly Minister of Finance in Argentina, is currently a professor of economics at the Argentinian Catholic University.

[1] See José Maria Dagnino Pastore, in *Economic Liberalization and Stabilization in the Southern Cone*, chapter 3 (Washington: World Bank, forthcoming); and Roque B. Fernandez and Carlos A. Rodriguez, *Inflacion y Estabilidad* (Buenos Aires: Ediciones Macchi, 1982).

- a significant jump in the total deficit of the public sector as a proportion of GDP after October 1980
- widespread virtual bankruptcy of enterprises, especially in manufacturing and construction, because of a sharp reduction in protection combined with overvaluation and very high real interest rates
- generalized illiquidity and insolvency of financial institutions
- the initial stages of a recessionary phase of the business cycle.

In short, the nation faced severe external imbalance as well as acute domestic recession as the government changed hands in March 1981. This situation, projected over time, loomed over successive governments and economic teams, forcing adjustment efforts long before any IMF intervention.

These brief notes attempt to tell the story of the adjustment efforts in two clearly different stages: pre- and post-Malvinas. They also offer a view of the prospects ahead.

PRE-MALVINAS ADJUSTMENT

The administration of General Roberto Eduardo Viola, inaugurated in March 1981, lacked the full support of the armed forces and looked unstable from the start. A new cabinet organization curtailed the powers of the ministry of economics to coordinate fiscal policy.

Dr. Lorenzo Sigaut's initial moves were a 30 percent devaluation of the peso, coupled with increased export taxes to cushion the impact on domestic prices, and the announcement that the exchange rate policy would roughly follow the purchasing power parity rule (PPP), based on an optimistic inflation forecast. No exchange or price controls were imposed. Other measures were promulgated to reduce the public deficit. An alleviation of the financial position of private firms was sought, by extending the maturities of their debts to the financial system.

Political and economic uncertainties, and limitations on action by the government and its economic team, resulted in continuous pressure on the external balance. The clear recovery of the balance of trade was more than offset by leads and lags in import and export payments, and gross capital outflows continued during the second quarter of 1981. Repeated runs on the peso forced successive devaluations, 18.3 percent monthly, until June, when a two-tier market was established. The collapse of the peso was largely the unavoidable consequence of overvaluation under the previous administration.

These events drove up the inflation rate, but its somewhat unexpected character left interest rates behind the wholesale price index (WPI)[2] (9.7 percent and 12.9 percent monthly); real wages and gross domestic product in the manufacturing sector (MGDP) declined even more sharply while GDP continued to fall. The rate of monetary expansion increased slightly during this period, driven by fiscal needs. The creation of separate commercial and financial exchange markets—without exchange controls—was accompanied by a system of exchange rate insurance for the repayment of medium-term (18-month) foreign credits while aimed at reducing exchange rate risk.

While market forces pulled the financial exchange rate up by 25.9 percent monthly, the officially regulated commercial exchange rate grew at 10.3 percent monthly, faster than domestic prices (CPI increased by 8.4 percent monthly). High demand for credit to buy dollars and a moderate pace of domestic credit creation caused real interest rates on loans to become positive again. The exchange insurance system was then (correctly) perceived as heavily subsidized and kept foreign funds flowing in. The trade balance was in surplus in the third quarter of 1981, yet its impact was not fully reflected in reserve changes due to the effect of leads and lags in payments. High real interest rates, together with sharply declining real wages accentuated the decline in MGDP and GDP.

The final quarter of 1981 was marked by increasing rumors (later confirmed) of a change toward a stronger government and austere economic policies. The relative gap between the financial and the commercial exchange rates narrowed slightly; the real exchange rate continued to depreciate while the interest rate fell in both nominal and real terms. Foreign trade showed a seasonally negative balance, but the lead-lag payments effect subsided. The fall in MGDP and GDP almost came to an end and real wages experienced a temporary improvement, while inflation diminished slightly (to 7.8 percent monthly CPI) keeping pace with the rate of monetary growth.

Thus the main events during the nine months of Sigaut's tenure were:

- a real depreciation, with a rise of the real exchange rate from 51.7 to 79.0 (1978 = 100), in spite of a terms of trade deterioration from 112.8 to 96.6

[2] When the prices of tradables rise faster than those of nontradables, WPI tends to exceed CPI growth.

- a return to trade balance surpluses and a reduction of the nine-month current account deficit from $4 billion to $2.6 billion, notwithstanding the increase in international interest rates
- a jump in the foreign debt to $35.7 billion (3.9 years of exports) of which 57 percent fell due in 1982, and a further drop in reserves
- accumulated declines of 8.8 percent in GDP; 15.2 percent in MGDP and 11.2 percent in real wages, and slightly rising employment
- a belated fall in bankruptcies, due to a lower real interest rate on loans and the (delayed) extension of debt maturities
- the maintenance of the consolidated public sector deficit at about 7.1 percent of GDP.

In broad terms the Argentinian economy experienced severe recession in 1981 as well as the trauma of extreme depreciation (as the peso lost two-thirds of its value relative to the dollar in nine months), while at the same time foreign debt continued to escalate because of continued external deficits and special incentives to borrow abroad.

Lieutenant General Leopoldo Fortunato Galtieri overthrew Viola in December 1981. He tried to build up an image of authority and to strengthen the ailing military régime. Full powers were restored to the ministry of economy, then under the charge of Dr. Roberto T. Alemann, whose explicit aims were to disinflate, to denationalize public enterprises, and to deregulate the economy.

Initially, the orthodox stabilization measures applied generated favorable price and exchange rate expectations. The exchange market was reunified and no exchange controls were imposed. Public wages, tariffs, and prices were frozen and credit to the private sector was increased more slowly.

The effects were almost to stop the exchange rate momentum during the first quarter of 1982—when it depreciated at only 2 percent monthly—and to reduce the inflation rate as measured by WPI. Following the devaluation of the commercial exchange rate implicit in the unification, the trade balance showed a first quarter surplus and the capital account was positive. Thus, the foreign sector no longer had a contractionary effect on money supply. However, the financial needs of public firms kept growing rapidly. The rate of monetary expansion was reduced to the rate of change in the WPI. GDP and MGDP showed a small, short-lived increase. But unemployment was on the rise and real wages fell 27.5 percent cumulatively, from the previous peak in the third quarter of 1980. Real interest rates on loans were persistently high: 21.2 percent in the previous 12 months. Bankruptcies hit a peak. The first general labor mobilization in years occurred at the end of March 1982.

The Alemann program was essentially a brisk turn toward fiscal-monetary orthodoxy, and whatever its ultimate success might have been, large groups of the public perceived its costs as high, leading to considerable political resistance (for example, to its imposition of a wage freeze in the public sector).

Then came the Malvinas. Quite surprisingly, its effect on most economic variables was relatively small, due to firm management. The restrictive fiscal policy led to a reduction in the rate of credit creation to 6 percent monthly, and a larger share of credit was oriented toward the private sector. Nominal interest rates remained steady. But the deepening of the recession continued: there were new sharp decreases in GDP, MGDP, and real wages.

A definitive policy change occurred: exchange controls and import licenses were imposed soon after the conflict broke. Expectations of the postwar scenario were apparent in the rise of the unregulated exchange rate (31.5 percent monthly) and of the WPI (15 percent) in June. Moreover, an important process was taking place in the world: international banks were reducing their exposure in developing countries. In the case of Argentina, the capital account turned from a positive balance to a $2.1 billion deficit in the second quarter of 1982. By now the external credit disruption associated with war added to the internal recession and remaining external current account deficits to complicate further Argentina's economic problems.

POST-MALVINAS ADJUSTMENTS

After the war ended, the Army required Galtieri's resignation, but the three commanders-in-chief could not agree on a presidential figure. Thus, the Army nominated General (ret.) Reynaldo Benito Antonio Bignone and the other two forces withdrew temporarily from the junta.

As his first action Bignone made a public commitment to hold elections and to hand over the government by March 1984 at the latest. The guidelines for economic policy were to make a public inventory of the situation and to prepare conditions to facilitate the success of the next administration. In order to understand the post-Malvinas economic policy, one must realize that this was not only the final phase of the military régime, but also a preparatory stage for a constitutional government.[3]

By mid-1982, Argentina's GDP had grown 2 percent since 1974; industrial output was at the 1960's level. The number of industrial workers was 23 percent lower than in 1970, and capacity utilization was at 63 percent. Consumption per capita had dropped 8 percent in the previous three years and unemployment was at 6 percent, the highest in the last five years. The widespread virtual bankruptcy of enterprises had not been solved, nor its consequences.

Foreign debt had climbed above $35.6 billion, annual interest payments were $4.5 billion, and Argentina was $2.5 billion in arrears. Public expenditures were still too high and in addition to the heavy public debt burden, crowded private borrowers out of the financial markets.

The new government's initial economic policy included the following elements:

- a partially compensated[4] devaluation, an extension of import control and payment regulations, the establishment of reference prices to avoid over- and underinvoicing of imports and exports, and a scheme to increase exports, to generate foreign exchange to service foreign debt and to sustain a reactivation of the economy
- an extension of the maturities and a reduction of the interest rates on business debts to the domestic financial system, in order to improve the flows of funds, the asset values, and the inventory level of firms
- a price behavior agreement with large enterprises, in exchange for additional financial advantages
- a financial reform, dividing the market into a regulated and a free segment
- creation of a two-tier (commercial and financial) exchange market, while maintaining exchange controls
- measures to reduce the burden to enterprises of their foreign debts
- gradual raising of charges for public services, budget reductions, and reductions in the interest burden of the public debt, to control the fiscal deficit.

Implementation of these policies achieved quick success in some aspects and went astray in others; on the whole the new strategy might

[3] Both of the economic teams of the Bignone administration consulted frequently with economists of the major parties and, as far as possible, incorporated their suggestions.
[4] By reducing subsidies and increasing taxes on exports.

have set the grounds for a process more acceptable to the major political parties.

The imposition of a ceiling on interest rates below previous levels provoked a rapid demonetization (from 25 percent to 19 percent during the third quarter of 1982). The outflow of funds from the financial system went into physical assets, foreign financial assets, and consumption goods. Demand was also stimulated by the increase in real wages (2.9 percent). As a result there were sharp reversals in some variables with respect to the previous quarter: MGDP grew 9.8 percent (compared to −7.6 percent); GDP grew by 1.3 percent (compared to −4.8 percent), while unemployment decreased markedly. In a dramatic step to alleviate the risk of widespread bankruptcy, the imposition of credit ceilings in the face of rapid domestic inflation caused a reduction in the real domestic debt of business by about 30 percent (in addition to the stretching-out of the debt, solving a pervasive problem).

A number of things went wrong. The financial reform left no attractive domestic financial assets available and therefore unnecessarily increased pressure on the unregulated exchange market. Interest rates soared 27 percent a month. The gap between this rate and the effective exchange rate for exporters sapped exports, via retention, underinvoicing, and smuggling.

The price behavior agreements were delayed and failed to avoid the sharp price increase of July, although they improved later on. Still, during the quarter the CPI rose 16 percent a month, although it showed a tendency to decline. In contrast to the tough wage policy under Alemann and Galtieri, the new government was not prepared to resist pressures for excessive nominal wage increase. The last two factors made the supply response inelastic, causing more inflation and less recovery than necessary.

The worsening of the current account of the balance of payments was compensated by strong efforts to obtain and renew foreign credits and to repay them by means of long-term bonds issued by the government. Thus, reserves remained essentially unchanged. Monetary expansion remained below 6 percent monthly, with a marked redistribution of credit to the private sector.

By comparison with the pre-Malvinas program of Alemann, the strategy adopted in mid-1982 was more eclectic and unorthodox. It set as a high priority the alleviation of domestic recession and aversion of widespread bankruptcy. It chose the path of price controls and effective domestic debt relief, and accepted larger wage increases than would have been countenanced under more orthodox approaches. It did succeed in temporary reactivation of a severely depressed economy, but at the cost of certain adverse effects such as reacceleration of inflation and deterioration in external accounts. Moreover, by the fourth quarter of 1983 it was evident that a key to resolving Argentina's external difficulties would be the achievement of an IMF-supported program of adjustment.

After the resignation of the economic team, Dr. Jorge Wehbe took charge of the ministry of economy.

The new team moved fast on three fronts. The foreign debt was refinanced through an IMF stand-by and a complementary package, which became possible after the mutual lifting of financial restrictions between Argentina and the United Kingdom. Negotiations began in September and were completed in December 1982. The commercial and financial exchange markets were reunified in two steps, the final one at the end of October. Last, the regulated interest rate was raised to levels compatible with the inflation rate.

As a result, in spite of a deterioration of both the current and the capital account of the balance of payments and of the fall in reserves, the relative gap between the unregulated and the commercial (later official) exchange rates narrowed to 37 percent (they grew at 5.3 percent and 18.8 percent monthly, respectively). Part of this was due to the slow expansion of the money supply (4.3 percent a month) and credit to the private sector. Real interest rates on loans and deposits were slightly positive and negative, respectively.

Both the reduction in the public sector debt burden and the export tax increase in July were kept, helping to maintain the reduction in the fiscal deficit. Real wages increased 17.2 percent during the fourth quarter of 1982. MGDP and GDP continued growing, though at a slower pace.

The IMF stabilization plan and the Wehbe economic strategy represented a partial swing back toward economic orthodoxy. Thus, the increase in interest rate ceilings meant a return of the capital market toward more normal savings flows, and the budgetary restraint undertaken in the IMF program represented a more traditional approach to reducing inflation than the program of price controls instituted in mid-1982.

By the end of the first quarter of 1983, the situation looked much better. Despite all the difficulties, economic performance is adapting to the political move to a constitutional government. The danger of default has subsided and Argentina is complying with the targets of the IMF stand-by (as of March 31) and pulling out of arrears. Balance of payments projections for 1983 (first quarter 1983 shows a $0.1 billion current account surplus) promise a reduction of the foreign debt in constant dollars and a much better maturity profile.[5] The real exchange rate is now at 126.6 (1978 = 100). The gap between the two exchange rates was 33 percent on March 31. The recovery of the foreign sector was more difficult because of a terms of trade deterioration from 90.1 to 82.9 (1978 = 100); but it was eased by the reduction of LIBOR (London interbank borrowing rate) from 15.4 percent to 9.4 percent annually—though partially compensated by the increase in the spreads of international bank credits to Argentina.

The danger of hyperinflation has also diminished sharply. The government has twice resisted pressures for excessive nominal wage increases (December 1982 and March 1983). The consolidated public sector deficit as compared with GDP dropped by more than half in 1982, to 3.3 percent.* The rate of money creation has been 6.7 percent a month during the first quarter of 1983. The rate of inflation has fallen steadily after stiffer price controls in early February.

The danger of a continued depression, bankruptcies, and financial collapses has disappeared, although higher real interest rates on loans might cause a recessionary phase of an inventory cycle. But unemployment is down to 3.7 percent and most GDP projections show a 2 percent to 4 percent rate of growth for 1983.

In short, progress under the Wehbe economic program with IMF support has been encouraging. External targets and domestic monetary targets have been met, and the partial return to orthodoxy appears to have been accomplished without causing a renewed decline in real output.

	Dec. 31, 1982	Dec. 31 1983
Total foreign debt (billion dollars)	38.7	39.8
Due next year (percentage)	49	24

* *Ed. Note*: The Argentinian definition of budget deficit excludes domestic interest. Under the IMF definition, the stabilization program calls for a reduction in the government deficit from 14 percent in 1982 to 8 percent in 1983, and 5 percent in early 1984. See, for example, *Financial Times*, 16 December 1982.

[5] External debt

SHORT-RUN PROSPECTS

The most important short-run prospects for the Argentinian economy are embodied in the summary of post-Malvinas adjustments, above. A more detailed and sequential description could run as follows. The foremost priority of economic policy is compliance with the IMF stand-by targets.

The effects of the monetary target depend on the demand for credit, a function of price and exchange rate expectations. April brought stability to those expectations: WPI grew 6.8 percent and the exchange rate gap narrowed to a record low of 20 percent. There are, however, reasons to expect the decline of inflation to level off: the behavior of public tariffs, prices, and wages and an eventual rebound of food prices. The unregulated exchange rate could also pick up again after a reduction of supply and an increase in demand after July. This would raise loan interest rates, causing a temporary sharp reduction of inventories but with little effect on consumption.

The effects of the fiscal target will be to avoid a stronger crowding out of the private sector from the financial markets. It will maintain pressure to increase public tariffs and prices in real terms, and it will force the government to resist pushes for more wages, expenditure, and investment. Total public expenditures are likely to continue declining in real terms.

The effects of the external target will be to avoid lags in the rate of devaluation of the official exchange rate and to induce policy measures to reduce the gap between the unregulated exchange rate and the effective exchange rate for exporters. Possibilities are: in one direction, a gradual reduction of export taxes; in the other direction, the use of the unregulated interest rate on loans to reduce the demand for dollars, on top of the regularization of payments abroad.

A likely sequence of events, then, is a leveling of the economic recovery in the second quarter, due to the inventory cycle and to a slowdown or reversal of the demonetization. Exports will be dynamic until July or August, and consumption is likely to continue on a slightly growing trend. Government expenditure and total investment will continue to decrease.

The third quarter is likely to witness a (seasonal) decline in exports, on top of the already mentioned behavior of prices and exchange rates. But real wages should keep growing or at least remain constant, sustaining consumption. Some speculative inventory accumulation might also occur toward the end.

Finally, the fourth quarter of 1983 might show price rises in anticipation of future controls, and a decline in real wages, with negative effects on consumption. While nominal interest rates are likely to increase, the same is not true for real rates.

Thus, the prospects are good for successful implementation of the IMF program, although with some risk that by the fourth quarter its internal targets could become jeopardized.

LONGER RUN PROSPECTS

Finally, a few words as to the longer run prospects of the Argentinian economy. It is practically certain that the constitutional government will be elected and inaugurated by January 1984.

Most observers foresee a polarization of votes toward the two major parties, the Justicialista and the Radical. In the last election, 10 years ago, the Justicialista reached almost 50 percent and the two parties together exceeded 70 percent of the ballots cast. Neither party is extreme, and both have a wide spectrum of wings and opinions. They have not selected their candidates yet, but their main leaders are moderate. Their platforms are also still to be prepared, but both parties have traditionally believed in a mixed (private and public) economy for Argentina—very much as it is today. It is, however, too early to assess which party will be the winner, who will be its leader and its chief economist, what coalitions and oppositions will be formed, and the resulting priorities and policies in economic matters.

Some observations may be made on the situation the new government will initially face. Although the rescheduling will take some pressures off the foreign debt, Argentina will need continued access to foreign credit: to roll over the principal due and secure additional moderate amounts of new funds. This highlights the importance of complying with the IMF targets. While the danger of hyperinflation might have subsided, the inflation rate seems likely to remain too high and therefore to pose a threat to stable economic progress. The fiscal situation will be better and could offer additional opportunities as a stabilization tool—more progressive taxation and cuts in military spending.

An important question to which the answer is still unclear concerns the role of the labor unions, both politically and in economic policy making. Investment (even foreign) projects are being delayed waiting for the inauguration of the new government.

A key question on which we may shed some light is the limitation to economic growth (a political must) imposed by the foreign sector. An exercise conducted using basic forecasts from other sources[6] shows that rates of growth in GDP of 4 percent in 1984 and of 5 percent in 1985 are likely to produce current account deficits of $1.2 billion and $1.4 billion, respectively, implying requirements of new foreign funds well within the probable behavior of the international financial community.

Argentina thus faces the transition to civilian rule with an economy making important gains from its extreme difficulties of 1981–82, when large external deficits, collapse in the exchange rate, domestic recession that provoked a wave of bankruptcies, and the breakdown of normal debt servicing meant one of the most severe economic crises Argentina has experienced. Performance under the new stabilization program shows considerable promise of success in terms of recovery of economic activity and improved external accounts, although progress against inflation has been less rapid. Normalization in the external sector is encouraging because Argentina will continue to need modest amounts of external finance for acceptable growth. The role of the labor unions and the potential for avoiding a reacceleration of still high inflation will be important determinants of the prospects for continued economic improvement as Argentina moves to civilian rule.

[6] Morgan Guaranty Trust Co. *World Financial Markets*, February 1983 for international financial aspects; *Econometrica SA* for the rest.

Appendix

FIGURE 1A.1 CURRENT ACCOUNT OF THE BALANCE OF PAYMENTS

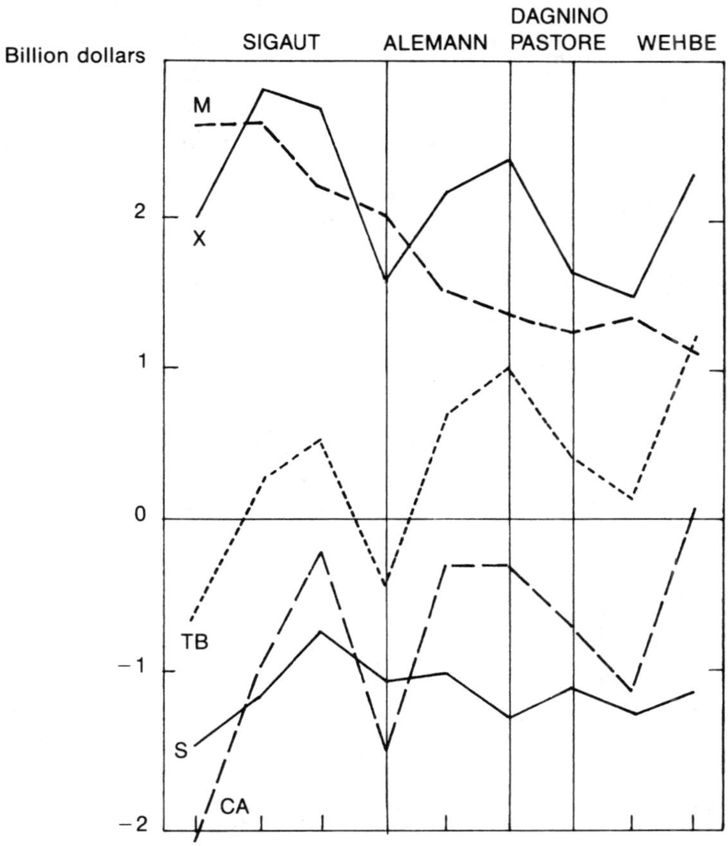

X Exports
M Imports
TB Trade Balance
S Services
CA Current Account

FIGURE 1A.2 EXCHANGE RATES AND TERMS OF TRADE

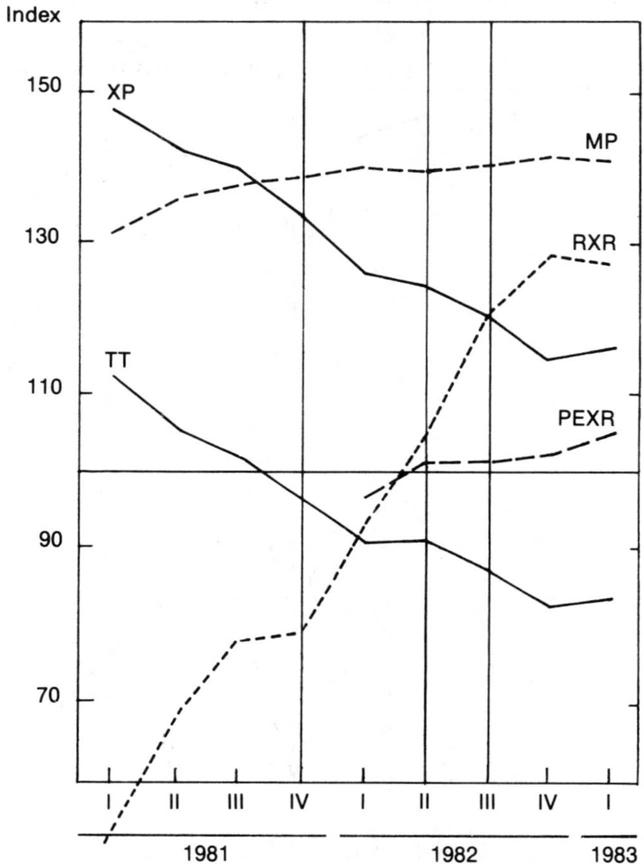

XP Export Prices (1978 = 100)
MP Import Prices (1978 = 100)
TT Terms of Trade (1978 = 100)
RXR Real Exchange Rate (1978 = 100)
PEXR Primary Effective Exchange Rate (Dec. 1981 = 100)

FIGURE 1A.3 CAPITAL ACCOUNT OF THE BALANCE OF PAYMENTS

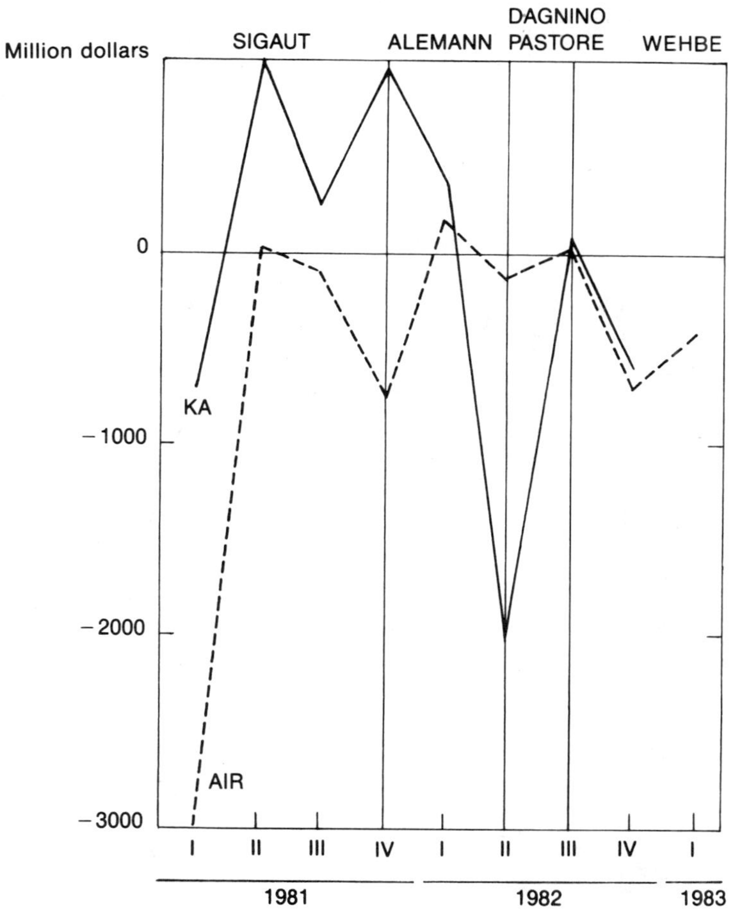

KA Noncompensatory Capital Movements
AIR Change in International Reserves

FIGURE 1A.4 REAL WAGES AND INTEREST

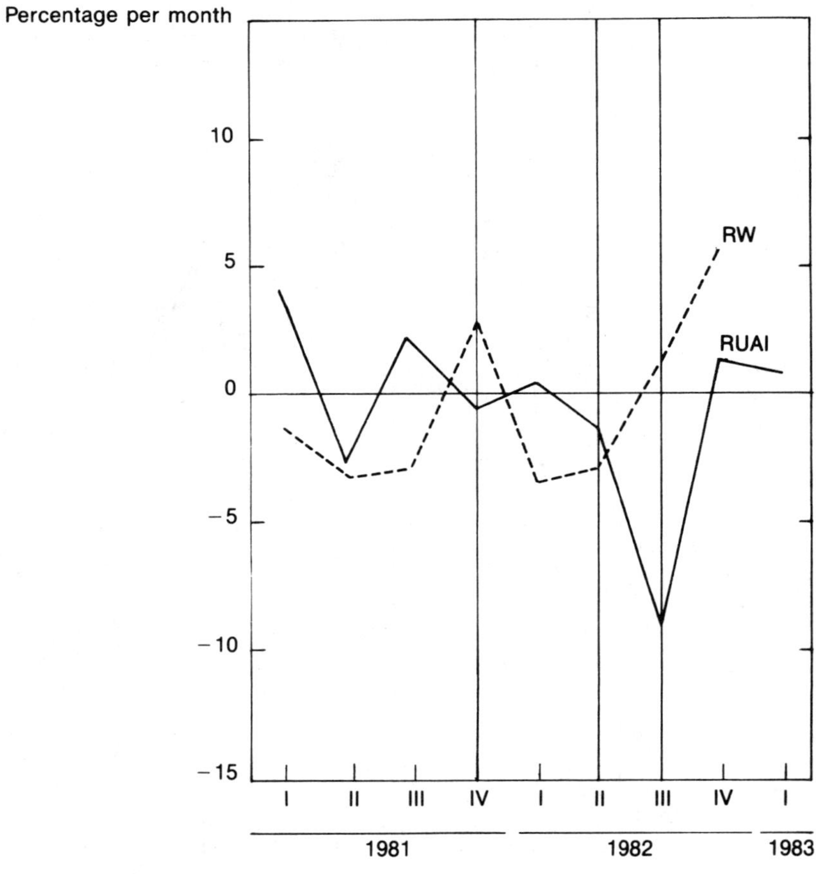

RW Change in Real Wage
RUAI Real Unregulated Interest Rate on Loans

FIGURE 1A.5 MONEY, PRICES AND INTEREST

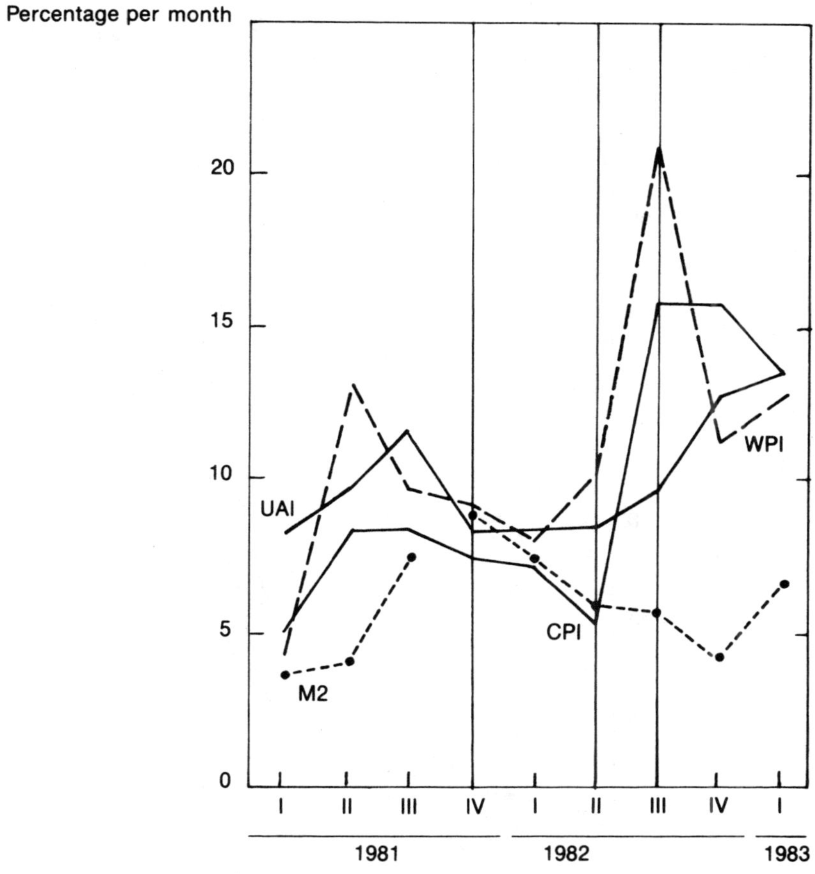

M2 Change in Monetary Resources
WPI Change in Wholesale Price Index
CPI Change in Consumer Price Index
NAI Unregulated Nominal Interest Rate on Loans

FIGURE 1A.6 NOMINAL EXCHANGE RATES

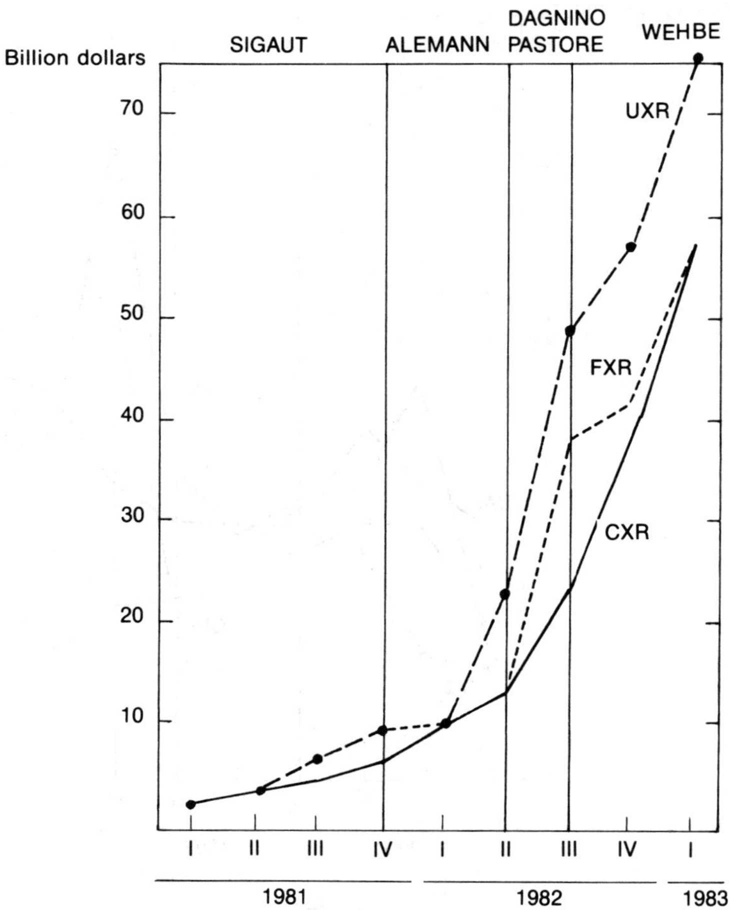

CXR Commercial Exchange Rate
FXR Financial Exchange Rate
UXR Unregulated Exchange Rate

TABLE 1A.1 REAL ACTIVITY IN ARGENTINA, 1981–83

Period	*GDP*	*MGDP*	*UR*
1981-I	−4.3	−5.7	n.a.
1981-II	−1.7	−7.0	4.0
1981-III	−5.6	−8.3	n.a.
1981-IV	−1.7	−0.8	5.0
1982-I	1.5	2.3	n.a.
1982-II	−4.8	−7.6	5.7
1982-III	1.3	9.8	n.a.
1982-IV	0.6	3.1	3.7
1983-I	n.a.	4.5[a]	n.a.

n.a. Not available; GDP Change in real gross domestic products (percentage per quarter); MGDP Change in real manufacturing gross domestic product (percentage per quarter); UR Unemployment rate-great Buenos Aires, percentage.
SOURCE: Econometrica SA databank, Buenos Aires.
a. Estimated.

Discussion

Miguel A. Kiguel

Dagnino Pastore has provided a very useful description of the recent evolution of the Argentinian economy. The discussion, however, lacks detail on the evolution of the external sector during this period and the causes of the balance of payments problems. This comment will attempt to analyze whether the difficulties in the external sector originated in domestic or foreign factors.

At the risk of being too taxonomic, I will argue that there was a first stage in which the external sector was disrupted by domestic policy decisions, while in the second stage the main problem was foreign disturbances.

During the Martinez de Hoz administration (April 1976–March 1981) the Argentinian economy underwent drastic structural changes, especially regarding its external sector. The level of tariff protection was significantly reduced, which greatly affected production and consumption patterns and the volume of international trade (which by the end of 1980 was triple that of 1977). The government also liberalized the domestic financial markets, and as part of that reform it authorized almost free international capital flows.

At the same time, the central bank followed a very controversial exchange rate policy. It fixed the rate of devaluation of the exchange rate at a much lower level than the going rate of inflation, a policy that finally led to a significant overvaluation of the domestic currency.

All these changes greatly affected the structure of the balance of payments. The reduction in trade restrictions and the overvaluation of the currency caused a record $10.5 billion level of imports during 1980, while exports remained at the previous year's $8 billion level. It also affected the capital account. Because there was free mobility of financial capital and the rate of devaluation plus the world nominal interest rate was much lower than the domestic nominal interest rate, there was a big inflow of capital, much of it highly speculative. Interest payments associated with this flow of capital caused a worsening of the current account balance.

When the Sigaut administration tried to correct the current account imbalance through an adjustment in the real exchange rate (as discussed in the paper), the economy was disturbed by international events. The world dollar interest rate rose to unprecedented levels (in both real and nominal terms), at the same time as the world economy experienced a deep recession, thus making it more difficult for Argentina to export its products. Finally, the terms of trade started to deteriorate (a trend that continued until the end of 1980) exerting an additional pressure on the external sector.

Despite these changes, the balance of trade remained roughly in equilibrium in 1981, but the economy was able to service its debt only by contracting new obligations. The external accounts —despite the Malvinas war—did not change drastically during the next year. The trade balance showed a surplus of $2.6 billion in 1982, with interest payments of approximately $6 billion. The stock of foreign debt reached $38 billion at the end of 1982.

From this brief discussion of the events that preceded what is now called the "external crisis" in Argentina, one gets the following impressions:

- After the real exchange rate had been adjusted and import restrictions implemented, the trade balance responded fairly quickly; despite the fall in the terms of trade and the world recession, the economy was able to maintain a trade surplus.
- The main problem for the economy was clearly derived from the external debt, and in particular from the contraction of short-term debt to finance consumption and long-term investment. The reserves were simply not there to repay these loans.

What are the prospects of a favorable solution to this problem? First, I consider that it is in the interests of both Argentina and the international banks to roll over this debt, and if possible to reschedule it for longer maturities.

Second, the economy should be able to meet the interest payments on the foreign debt. Imports have been significantly reduced, while exports are expanding due to the exceptionally good harvest. The projected trade balance seems to be better than previously predicted and the estimates for the current account in 1983 are extremely favorable. The outlook will be even better given a world recovery and lower interest rates.

Let me now address the specific questions prepared for this conference. The first one regards the size of the financial resources provided by the IMF. I think that for the Argentinian case they were adequate, at least they seem to have been adequate ex post.

Regarding the size of the import restrictions I do not think that they have been too severe. Real GDP in 1982 remained at the 1977 level, while imports last year were much smaller in real terms. Thus, there seems to be scope to increase output and imports without destabilizing the trade balance.

How likely is the risk of default? On present trends, I do not foresee any major debt-service problem. However, the economy is still in a "marginal" position and even a small increase in the world interest rate could disturb the economy. The authorities will need to maintain restraint in domestic policies affecting the current account. This might be difficult during a general election year. International bankers will also need to show restraint in their interest rate to Argentina, since the prospects of an external recovery depend greatly on the ability to meet interest payments without contracting new debt.

A default by any one of these three countries would certainly disrupt world economic and financial markets. Many of the loans to Argentina, Brazil, and Mexico have been channeled through the Eurodollar market, where deposits are of very short term and not insured. Thus, any loss in confidence could quickly lead to a run on the banks and a world financial crisis. This would not further anyone's interest.

In conclusion, some lessons should be drawn from the Argentinian experience. First, a country should avoid long and persistent fluctuations in the real exchange rate, which in most cases affect the structure of production as well as the pattern of financing debt. Second, the recent exchange rate policy (which was also followed by Chile and Uruguay) tends to support the view that unrestricted financial capital flows can be a destabilizing force in a small open economy that fixes the exchange rate.

2 The IMF and the Prospects for Adjustment in Brazil

Edmar L. Bacha

This paper discusses the short-term economic prospects for Brazil in the context of the adjustment program that the Brazilian authorities have adopted, with the support of the International Monetary Fund (IMF).

The short-term balance of payments problems of the country are reviewed in the following section. Section three discusses the content and perspectives of the domestic targets of the adjustment program. On the basis of this analysis tentative suggestions are put forward, related to the establishment of domestic performance criteria in IMF sponsored adjustment programs. The paper concludes with a discussion of alternative short-term forecasts for the Brazilian economy.

BALANCE OF PAYMENTS

Brazil's overall balance of payments deficit was nearly $9 billion in 1982. During the last quarter of that year, net international reserves turned negative; at year-end their value cannot have been higher than *minus* $2.5 billion.[1] Recently, the Brazilian central bank (CB) acknowl-

---

Professor Bacha is a professor of economics at the Pontifícia Universidade Católica do Rio de Janeiro. *The author gratefully acknowledges research support from PNPE/IPEA.*

[1] The IMF Staff Report of February 10, 1983, reproduced in Galveas, puts this value at *minus* $1.5 billion, assuming a balance of payments deficit of $7.5 billion. Subsequently, Struckmeyer and Reichmann raised the IMF estimated deficit to $8.9 billion, implying a much larger drain than had been previously allowed for on Brazil's net international reserve position.

edged that its cash position in convertible currencies was a meager $658 million on December 31, 1982.[2]

For a desperate problem, a desperate solution. At the end of October, the Brazilian government announced an emergency foreign sector program expressing its firm commitment to generate at all costs a $6 billion trade surplus in 1983 (compared with a surplus of $800 million in 1982).[3]

With the temporary support of bridge-loans from the US Treasury, the Bank for International Settlements (BIS), and a small group of large banks, the Brazilian authorities hurriedly negotiated a loan package for 1983 with the private international banking community and the IMF, designed to stop the drain on Brazil's international reserves.

On the basis of an extended arrangement, the IMF committed itself to a loan total of $2.5 billion during 1983. The banks for their part were requested to (1) disburse $4.4 billion of new loans in 1983; (2) roll over $4.7 billion of amortization due in 1983 on medium- and long-term debt; (3) maintain existing trade credits, at levels variously estimated between $8.8 and $9.6 billion; and (4) reestablish deposits in Brazilian banks abroad that were withdrawn in mid-1982 (these withdrawals were guess-estimated by the Brazilian authorities to have been nearly $3.0 billion[4]). Projects (1) and (2) were signed in New York in late February, while two groups of banks were assigned the thankless task of guaranteeing observance of projects (3) and (4).

After signature of these loan agreements, the finance minister, in a speech to the Brazilian Congress, proclaimed that the apparently intractable balance of payments problem of the country had been solved.[5] A few weeks later, however, the CB admitted that it was in arrears by $1 billion and that this negative cash position would not reverse itself, at least until September.[6] The CB governor also said that this was a transitory phenomenon, due to the seasonal pattern of the trade account and the heavy concentration of repayments of the bridge operations in the first half. Tentative new month-by-month projections of the balance of payments were presented to the banks charged with liaison. Less

---

[2] Telegram to the Liaison Banks (April 17, 1983) as reproduced in *Gazeta Mercantil*, 3 May 1983.

[3] Cf. Banco Central do Brasil (1982a).

[4] Galveas, p. 57.

[5] Cf. Galveas.

[6] Cf. telegram. All data in this paragraph as reproduced in *Gazeta Mercantil*, 3 May 1983.

optimistic assumptions were adopted about new trade credits, direct investment, intra-firm loans, and other long-term capital. However, the CB governor found it "too soon" to abandon the $6.0 billion target for the trade surplus. In spite of these changes, the CB still considered it possible to close the accounts with a nonnegative cash position on December 31.

Independent observers do not concur. Paulo N. Batista, Jr., estimates financing requirements for 1983 that are at least $4 billion higher than projected by the CB. The *Amex Bank Review* thinks that further finance of $3 billion to $5 billion will be required. The *Economist* reckons that Brazil "may be back before the end of the year looking for anything up to $4 billion."

Were the loan packages adopted appropriate to the needs of the situation, given the scale of the financial resources available and the state of the world economy? Clearly not. Even if the accounts are balanced just in time for New Year's Eve, as the CB seems to expect, right now the country is in arrears. And the sums in arrears are expected to continue increasing until next July.[7] The CB has already admitted that in the rushed negotiations of late last year, the seasonality of the trade accounts and the concentration of repayments of the short-term bridges were disregarded. Additionally, the CB seems to have seriously underestimated the extent of the drying up of interbank deposits in Brazilian banks abroad, as well as the degree of retrenchment of short-term trade credits.

There is now a widespread feeling that the Brazilian authorities were ill-advised to attempt to force the banks to swallow projects (3) and (4), whose failure has faced them with the need for a new renegotiation after only a few months. Nowadays, cashless, the authorities' only hope is that the pressure of accumulating unpaid bills will succeed in driving more money out of the banks, before trade flows start to stall.

What would be the consequences of a disruption of trade flows, caused by a refusal of the banks to keep discounting Brazilian trade bills? Serious indeed. Brazil does not have any cash in hand, and domestic oil stocks are said to correspond to less than two months' consumption.[8] In the absence of trade credit, the country could continue functioning only with strict rationing schemes and severe price controls.

---

[7] Cf. telegram.

[8] Cf. José Roberto Alencar, "Petróleo: os estoques brasileiros não foram sacrificados à balança," *Gazeta Mercantil*, 5 May, 1983.

Interest payments and other foreign capital remittances would naturally be immediately suspended, and this action could easily provoke a financial panic abroad. This is an inconceivable scenario, if a minimum of political rationality prevails in international relations.

The question may then be asked whether stricter conditionality should not accompany a larger loan commitment, in the forthcoming round of debt renegotiations. This is not a rhetorical question, because Brazil's current IMF program is way off course, and it is certain not to meet the agreed targets.

DOMESTIC TARGETS

Brazil agreed with the Fund on very stringent fiscal performance criteria. The domestic credit of the monetary authorities was allowed by the program to increase by 63 percent, from December 1982 to December 1983. However, the public sector borrowing requirement (PSBR) was frozen in 1983 at the same *nominal* level as in 1982.[9] The latter target was difficult enough to fulfill with the 85 percent to 90 percent inflation rate projected for 1983 in the program. Meeting either of the targets is out of the question under the 8.5 percent monthly inflation rate observed from January to April.[10]

Extrapolated to December, this January to April inflation pattern implies a 172 percent 12-month price rise. The econometric model at Pontifícia Universidade Católica do Rio de Janeiro (PUC/RJ) tentatively estimates an average yearly inflation rate of 153 percent to 156 percent in 1983, even under the assumptions that (1) the new wage-curbing law now before Congress is approved; (2) direct price control measures are made slightly more effective; and (3) contrary to a Brazilian commitment under the IMF program, the rhythm of minidevaluations is decelerated a little.[11]

With an inflation rate of 150 percent, the net *real* domestic credit of the monetary authorities would contract by 35 percent during 1983, if the IMF program were applied as written in the February 24 Letter of Intent. The effect on the PSBR would be even more spectacular. To see this, first note that about one half of the PSBR is related to the service of domestic public debt.[12] Nearly all of this corresponds either

---

[9] February 24, 1983, Letter of Intent. Reproduced in Galveas.

[10] Inflation rates measured by the Vargas Foundation General Price Index.

[11] Cf. Carneiro, Modiano, Lopes, and Pinto.

[12] This value was estimated on the basis of the following quotation: "The IMF approach is much more encompassing and thus shows a higher deficit, i.e., nearly 14 percent of

to the "monetary correction" of the outstanding value of long-term government bonds, or to the inflation-related discount on the face value of government bills. Let us assume that these inflation factors account for 90 percent of total debt service. Assume further that the government will apply a "monetary correction" factor of only 80 percent of the actual inflation rate (and, correspondingly, that the discount factor on government bills will account for only 80 percent of actual inflation). Applying these coefficients to the estimated 150 percent inflation rate, the conclusion follows that the one-half of the PSBR which corresponds to debt service will increase by slightly over 100 percent in nominal terms in 1983. The other half—which we can denominate the inflation-corrected PSBR—then would have to decline to *zero* to keep the overall PSBR constant in nominal terms. In Struckmeyer and Reichmann, the overall PSBR is estimated to have been 16.9 percent of GDP in 1982. Half of this, or 8.5 percent, corresponds to the inflation-corrected PSBR. Bringing this down to zero would mean slashing Brazilian GDP by over 15 percent (assuming an income multiplier of about two, as suggested in recent research[13]). It might be done, under a dictatorship. Fortunately for the Brazilians, the process of political liberalization of the military régime seems to have already made enough progress to guarantee that such an economic prospect is highly improbable.

This critique of the IMF domestic currency targets for Brazil should not be read as condoning an inflation rate of 150 percent a year, or as implying that a country (even Brazil!) can function permanently under such a rate of monetary depreciation. However, the observation should be made that practical experience, theoretical models, and econometric estimates all concur in the conclusion that the inertia built into Brazilian inflation by both mandatory and customary indexation schemes *cannot* be bent by fiscal and monetary stringency, except at extremely high costs in terms of unemployment and forgone output.[14]

A subsequent question then would be whether the Fund could not have a constructive role to play in contributing to the establishment of

GDP in 1982, compared to 6.1 percent under the Brazilian approach. The bulk of the difference between the IMF and Brazilian measures is the indexation requirement on public debt, a fiscal overhang about which the authorities can do little or nothing in the short run. Excluding all public debt operations, the IMF figure is about 7 percent for 1982." Banco Central do Brasil (1982b), p. 12.

[13] Cf. Meira.

[14] The relevent theoretical models are collected in Taylor. The Brazilian experience is reviewed in several of the papers in Arida. Modiano provides a state-of-the-art econometric discussion.

a new incomes policy in the country. Such a supply-side attack on inflation could limit the amount of excess supply entailed by a contractionary fiscal and monetary policy. The Fund seems to have exerted a beneficial political influence along these lines in the cases of Italy and Great Britain during the 1970s. It can be guessed that, at some point in the future evolution of political liberalization of the country, the Fund might play such a role in Brazil. However, under the current transitional political situation, the Fund would only enhance its "wicked witch" image if it insisted on wage deindexation.[15]

Before the next Presidential term begins, in March 1985, one cannot expect much to be done about inflation, except ad hoc attempts to maintain it at its new plateau of 150 percent a year, by various devices that are within the grasp of the present government. This expectation needs to be qualified by the observation that Brazilians have never before lived under inflation of 150 percent. It might be that a threshold is being crossed, beyond which hyperinflation becomes a real possibility. This might occur because inflation currently has a strong negative effect on the current account of the monetary authorities, because of the credit subsidies extended to agriculture and exports. Real interest rates on these credits are inversely related to the inflation rate. The higher is the inflation the lower is the share of a given real credit expansion that can be financed out of the monetary authorities' current receipts. Hence, the higher is the share that needs to be ultimately supplemented by a real expansion of the monetary base. However, if this is the phenomenon that may eventually cause a hyperinflation in Brazil, the medicine is at hand, namely, a rise in the nominal interest rate on the subsidized credit. If this could not be done, then the situation would indeed be hopeless.

PERFORMANCE CRITERIA

A few consequences for the establishment of local currency denominated performance criteria seem to follow.

First, it is the inflation-corrected PSBR which should be used as a guide to policy. The use of the inflation-charged IMF concept may serve ill-hidden ideological purposes but only at the cost of the professional reputation of the Fund staff.[16]

---

[15] See Diaz-Alejandro for a fuller discussion of these topics.

[16] This still oversimplifies the problems involved in choosing an adequate budget deficit concept. For a fuller discussion, see Buiter.

Second, the cruzeiro-denominated criteria, particularly the net domestic credit expansion of the monetary authorities, should not be used as indirect ways of inflation targeting, for the simple reason that they are very ineffective instruments to control inflation in Brazil. Perhaps, an *explicit* inflation target should have been part of the performance criteria. Then, both the net domestic credit and the inflation-corrected PSBR would be fixed as a function of this target rate (with the caveat that all important sources of government income were appropriately sheltered against inflation).

Third, an additional hope would be that the Fund would seriously take into account the distinction between external and internal balance, explicitly incorporating into its analysis the possibility that exports might

TABLE 2.1 BRAZIL'S ADJUSTMENT PROGRAM: BASIC DATA FOR 1983.

	1982	*January–March 1983*	*1983*
IMF Performance Criteria			
Limit on borrowing requirement of nonfinancial public sector (trillion cruzeiros)	8.7	2.8	8.8
Limit on expansion of net domestic assets of monetary authorities (trillion cruzeiros)	5.1	6.2	8.3
Cumulative changes in net international reserves position of monetary authorities (billion dollars)	−2.5[a]	−1.5	—
Limit on expansion of net external debt (billion dollars)	82.8[a]	3.0	6.0
Performance and forecasts			
Inflation rate (percentage)	100	—	—
IMF	—	—	85/90
PUC	—	—	153/156
GDP growth rate (percentage)	0.5	—	—
IMF	—	—	−3.5
PUC	—	—	−1.5/−2.5
Trade balance (billion dollars)	0.8	—	—
CB	—	—	6.0
PUC	—	—	4.7/5.9
Exports, f.o.b. (billion dollars)	20.2	—	—
CB	—	—	22.0
PUC	—	—	21.2/22.4
Imports, f.o.b. (billion dollars)	19.4	—	—
CB	—	—	16.0
PUC	—	—	16.1/16.5
of which, oil (billion dollars)	9.6	—	—
CB	—	—	7.6
PUC	—	—	7.8/7.9
CB cash position (billion dollars)	0.7	—	—

— Not applicable.

SOURCES: Galveas; Carneiro; Lopes; Modiano; and Pinto.

a. Author's estimates.

effectively be constrained by external demand.[17] This would require the Fund staff to abandon its futile attempt to control the current account by imposing constraints on the PSBR. This attitude is related to its bad habit of inferring the value of the current account from the difference between domestic savings and investment. In the world economic conditions that we are currently facing, so clearly dictated by aggregate demand and credit constraints, it is a little exasperating to read the following in the opening paragraph of the IMF summary of the Brazilian program: "I. *Targets*. 1. An increase in domestic savings from 14.5 percent of GDP in 1982 to nearly 16 percent in 1983. . . . This would allow a reduction in the current account deficit from 4.5 percent of GDP in 1982 to 2.2 percent in 1983. . . ."[18] It is blatant that in the early 1980s the Brazilian current account is not constrained by an inadequate domestic saving rate. With current record levels of unemployment and slack capacity, there is plenty of room in the Brazilian economy for savings to increase together with income led by exports, if the world economy recovered and foreign protectionism abates. *Ceteris paribus*, an autonomous improvement in the domestic savings rate would only reduce the value of the income multiplier and thus decrease employment and capacity utilization rates even further, with only indirect consequences for the trade balance.

The above is not an excuse for the current low level of the domestic savings rate in Brazil, much less a justification for the deterioration of this coefficient since the late 1970s.[19] The point is simply that currently

---

[17] Analytical details of this view are explored in Bacha.

[18] Translated from the Appendix IV of the February 11, 1983, Staff Report, reproduced in Galveas.

[19] It is, however, likely that the IMF Staff Report reproduced in Galveas overestimates both the decline in the real savings rate in Brazil and the increase of the difference between domestic savings and investment since 1977. For the ratio of nominal savings to nominal GDP, which is the concept that the IMF apparently uses, can easily be shown to be a negative function of the ratio of foreign capital income to GDP and a positive function of the terms of trade. We start from the national accounts identity in current cruzeiros:

$$S = Sp + T - G$$

where: S = domestic savings, Sp = private savings, T = net taxes and other current receipts of the government, and G = government consumption expenditures. Dividing through by nominal GDP, Y, after manipulation we obtain:

$$S/Y = (1 - V/Y - t)(1 - P^{\alpha}.C_r/Y_{p,r}) + t - P^{\gamma}.G_r/Y_r$$

where V is foreign capital income, in current cruzeiros; P = terms of trade; C_r = real unemployed resources abound in the country because of the foreign exchange constraint. Hence, a program for recovery, while it should include measures to raise the domestic savings rate, should simultaneously worry about export promotion and import substitution, and about appropriate incentives to raise the fixed investment rate.

SHORT-TERM PERSPECTIVES

The arguments in the previous section suggest that more austerity ("stricter conditionality") is not the answer for Brazil's current financial plight. We also discussed what the IMF should be doing, which is not necessarily what it is doing. Hence, there is the possibility that the Fund will want to force Brazil to comply with the agreed performance criteria, even though perhaps in a slightly less strict fashion than written in the February 24 Letter of Intent.

This is a possible explanation of the fact that since last April the CB has followed an open market policy explicitly designed to raise the level of short-term interest rates, contrary to widely held expectations that an easier monetary policy would be adopted after the February maxidevaluation. Perseverance with this policy could indeed provoke an even deeper recession than the 3.5 percent GDP drop anticipated by the Fund for 1983. This might cause a further decline in the value of imports, beyond the 17.5 percent drop from 1982 to 1983 which is already part of the government program. Provided that export supply costs were not negatively affected by a generalized economic slump, such self-flagellation would then be rewarded by a large trade surplus.

---

private consumption; $Y_{p,r}$ = private sector real disposable income; t = net tax ratio to GDP; G_r = real government consumption expenditures; Y_r = real GDP; α = share of direct and indirect imports in private consumption; γ = share of direct and indirect imports in government consumption; and where it is implicitly assumed that the cruzeiro price of exports is equal to the GDP price deflator. By the same token, the ratio between nominal investment and nominal GDP is a negative function of the terms of trade:

$$I/Y = P^{\beta}.I_r/Y_r$$

where I is nominal investment; I_r, real investment; β is the share of direct and indirect imports in investment; and Y_r is real GDP. Now, since 1977, both the terms of trade deteriorated and the share of foreign capital increased continuously. Hence, the ratio of real savings to real GNP is underestimated and the ratio of real investment to GDP is overestimated when they are respectively approximated by the coefficients S/Y and I/Y, as the Fund staff seems to do. For a fuller discussion, see Bacha and Malan.

Ironically, according to preliminary macroeconomic projections at PUC/RJ,[20] there is now a fair chance that at year-end the Brazilian authorities may come close to fulfilling their trade surplus target. This could be achieved under current policies (as a consequence of the drop of oil prices and the favorable effects of the February maxidevaluation) and without a major domestic recession, provided that: international trade grows no less than 3 percent this year; the coffee and soybean crops are as good as currently expected by the ministry of agriculture; and sufficient additional domestic credit is made available to guarantee the commercialization of the bumper coffee and soybean crops without crowding out other income-generating activities.

This relatively favorable scenario may not occur for a number of reasons, unrelated to the new round of debt renegotiations that Brazil will soon be entering with the banks and the Fund. But it would be a pity if this scenario were not given a chance to materialize, because monetarist fundamentalism and antigovernment intervention ideology were to prevail over common sense in these negotiations, forcing Brazil into a deeper recession than it is currently experiencing as a consequence of past domestic and foreign policy mistakes.

REFERENCES

THE AMEX BANK REVIEW. 1983. "Latin America in Crisis: Common Themes and Diverse Experience." April 25.

ARIDA, PERSIO, ed. 1982. *Divida Externa, Recessao e Ajuste Estrutural: o Brasil Diante da Crise.* Rio de Janeiro: Paz e Terra.

BACHA, EDMAR L. Forthcoming. "Growth with limited supplies of foreign exchange: a reappraisal of the two gap model." In M. Syrquin, L. Taylor, and L. Westphal, eds., *Economic Structure and Performance* (essays in honor of Hollis Chenery). New York: Academic Press.

BACHA, EDMAR L. AND PEDRO MALAN. Forthcoming. "Brazil's debt: from the Miracle to the Fund." Pontifícia Universidade Católica do Rio De Janeiro.

BATISTA, PAULO N., JR. 1983. "A renegociação da divida externa brasileira." Processed. CEMI/IBRE/FGV. February.

BANCO CENTRAL DO BRASIL. 1982a. Programação do Setor Externo em 1983. Brasília: Conselho Monetário Nacional. October 25.

——— 1982b. "Brasil: Adjustment to the International Economy and External Financing Needs." Brasília: Conselho Monetario Nacional. December 20.

[20]Cf. Carneiro, Modiano, Lopes and Pinto. Some of these forecasts are summarized in table 2.1.

BUITER, WILLEM. 1982. "Deficits, Crowding Out and Inflation: The Simple Analytics." Discussion Paper no. 143. London: Centre for Labour Economics. London School of Economics. December.

CARNEIRO, DIONISIO, EDUARDO MODIANO, FRANCISCO LOPES, AND FRANCISCO PINTO. Forthcoming. "Acompanhamento macroeconômico da economia brasileira—1983/II." Pontifícia Universidade Católica do Rio de Janeiro.

DIAZ-ALEJANDRO, C. 1982. "The LDCs in the 1982 International Economy: Two Comments." Textos para Discussão no. 32. Economics Department, Pontifícia Universidade Católica do Rio de Janeiro.

THE ECONOMIST. 1983. "Latin America: the Breaking of a Continent." April 20, p. 27.

GALVEAS, ERNANE. 1983. "A Crise Mundial e a Estratégia Brasileira de Ajustamento do Balanço de Pagamentos" (Exposição do Ministro de Estado da Fazenda no Senado Federal em 23.3.83.). Brasília, March 23.

MEIRA, JERÓNIMO. 1983. "Crescimento Econômico e Estrangulamento Externo." Unpublished MA thesis. Economics Department, Pontifícia Universidade Católica do Rio de Janeiro.

MODIANO, EDUARDO. 1983. "A dinámica de salarios e preços na economia brasileira, 1966/81." Textos para Discussão no. 45. Economics Department, Pontifícia Universidade Católica do Rio de Janeiro.

STRUCKMEYER, HORST AND THOMAS REICHMANN. 1983. "Brazil Seeks to Strengthen External Position and Re-evaluate Strategy for Resumed Growth." *IMF Survey*. March 21.

TAYLOR, LANCE. Forthcoming. *Structuralist Macroeconomics*. New York: Academic Press.

Discussion

Rudiger Dornbusch

The discussion of Brazil's adjustment under the International Monetary Fund (IMF) stand-by program is very timely. The December program, hastily put together under US pressure, to prevent chaos in world financial markets, has come apart. Negotiations are pending for the next round. The question, of course, is whether conditionality should be *stricter*, whatever that means, or entirely different. Edmar Bacha's treatment of the issues is congenial, although it leaves room for disagreement with his assessment of the IMF and some of his specific ideas on policy. But there can be little disagreement with his call for incomes policy as a basic building block of stabilization policy. This is a point that Mario Simonsen and others have emphasized for some time, and it is good to see Bacha joining that position.[1]

Perhaps the most interesting aspect of Bacha's presentation is the absence of any discussion of renegotiation of the external debt—moratoria, partial debt write-offs, negotiation of spreads and terms—which might well be mentioned in this context. Instead of arguing that the debt is too burdensome, Bacha advances the striking proposition that, with moderate growth in real debt, Brazil will be able to finance its external

---

Dr. Dornbusch is professor of economics at the Massachusetts Institute of Technology, Cambridge, Mass.

[1] See M. Simonsen, "The Theory and Practice of Indexation in Brazil," in *Inflation, Debt and Indexation*, ed. R. Dornbusch and M. Simonsen (Cambridge, Mass.: MIT Press, 1983) and R. Dornbusch, "Stabilisation Policy in Developing Countries: What Lessons Have We Learnt?" *World Development* (September 1982).

balance, and even do so without a deep depression of economic activity. But he also notes that, forecasts apart, there are risks of hyperinflation or a collapse of activity. Hyperinflation could arise under the current course of policy whereas recession would be the almost certain outcome of compliance with the IMF's conditions on the public sector deficit.

GROWTH, INFLATION, AND THE EXTERNAL BALANCE

Table 1 shows data for Brazilian growth and for components of the external accounts in recent years. The data show clearly the policy blunder of 1979–80: in the face of a second oil shock and of growth in debt, a high growth strategy was maintained.

TABLE 1 BRAZIL: GROWTH AND THE EXTERNAL BALANCE (ANNUAL AVERAGES)

	1971–73	1974–78	1979–80	1981	1982
GDP growth (percentage change)	12.5	7.0	7.3	−1.9	−1.2
Current account deficit (billion dollars)	1.5	6.2	11.8	11.7	12.5
Exports (billion dollars)	4.6	10.3	17.7	23.3	20.2
Interest payments (billion dollars)	0.5	2.2	6.5	10.3	10.7
Oil imports (billion dollars)	0.5	3.5	8.1	11.0	10.2

SOURCE: Data Resources, Inc., Lexington, Mass.

Moreover, the implications of a shift toward tight money in the United States for *real* interest rates, for the real value of the dollar, commodity prices, and world trade were certainly not understood in Brasília. Policymakers there, who actually believed they would gain from disinflation, had completely the wrong estimate of the external repercussions of tight money in the United States. In December 1980 Delfim Netto actually urged the United States on in its fight against inflation, arguing[2]:

> It would be very important for us. Even if it were done at the cost of some reduction in the level of activity in the United States, this would be more helpful for us than an increase in exports. If you reduced rates because of a very responsible monetary policy, it is the same as if you increased our exports, because the current account deficit would be cut.

The stand-by agreement commits Brazil to a radical adjustment. Inflation that ran 100 percent last year is to fall below 80 percent already

---

[2] Antonio Delfim Netto, "We Cannot Afford A Big Recession" (interview), *Newsweek* (Latin American edition), 22 December 1980.

in 1983. The trade balance is to show a $6 billion surplus, net reserve changes are to be zero, and the public sector deficit is to decline by one-half (table 2).

TABLE 2 BRAZIL: KEY POLICY TARGETS
(percentage of GDP)

	1980	1981	1982	1983[a]	1984[a]
Inflation (annual percentage rate)	110.2	95.2	99.7	87.0	40.0
External debt	22.1	23.8	25.4	26.6	26.5
Public sector borrowing	7.5	12.7	16.9	8.8	5.5
Current account deficit	4.4	3.6	4.5	2.2	1.5

SOURCE: *IMF Survey*, March 21, 1983, p. 93
a. Planned

What are the chances that these targets can be met? There is no possibility at all of meeting the inflation target. With pervasive indexation and the cost and price shocks caused by devaluation and public sector price adjustments, inflation will certainly exceed 100 percent and will likely approach 150 percent. Right away this means that the proposed targets for domestic credit creation are unrealistic since they would imply a dramatic cut in the real money supply, beyond the 35 percent to 40 percent contraction of the last two years.

Bacha rightly argues that a cut in the public sector deficit by an amount equal to 8 percent of GDP is inconceivable. Without an extraordinary surge in exports, such a cut would imply a politically infeasible and economically unjustifiable depression of proportions not even remotely intended by the policymakers. The more likely outcome is, as Bacha suggests, a combination of recession, induced by the incredibly high real interest rates, and real depreciation, which provide some leeway on the external balance side. Such measures would relieve the immediate need for a thoroughgoing adjustment program, but would merely postpone the stabilization program, and thereby risk destroying the economic and social progress of the last decade.

BACHA AND THE IMF

Bacha's criticism of IMF policies centers mainly on two points: domestic credit ceilings as a concealed disinflation weapon, and a deflationary emphasis on saving as the source of external balance gains that ignores export constraints.

Bacha argues that the inflation-corrected public sector deficit, not the raw deficit, should figure in the performance criteria. This is explained by the conventional Bailey-Siegel argument that the proper measure of the public sector deficit (or of any deficit) is the change in the real value of the public sector's liabilities. Let B and P be the domestic currency liabilities (debt and highpowered money) and the price level and E and B^* the exchange rate and the foreign currency denominated debt. Then the change in the real value of government liabilities is:

$$(1) \quad \Delta\frac{(B + EB^*)}{P} = \frac{\Delta B + E\Delta B^*}{P} + \frac{EB^*}{P}\left(\frac{\Delta E}{E} - \frac{\Delta P}{P}\right) - \frac{B}{P}\frac{\Delta P}{P}$$

$$= \underset{\text{deficit}}{\text{Raw}} + \underset{\text{debt adjustment}}{\text{Foreign currency}} - \underset{\text{adjustment.}}{\text{Inflation}}$$

Bacha stresses the need to correct the budget for inflation, noting that part of government outlays are nominal interest payments for amortization, not debt service. But according to the same logic the capital gains or losses on the external debt arising from changes in real exchange rates must be taken into account. Thus, any real depreciation ($\Delta E/E - \Delta P/P > 0$) would tend to increase the corrected deficit. The same logic that would reduce raw deficits by the inflation adjustment would then have to increase them by a possible external adjustment.

But there is a more basic issue: what is the budget target all about? There are two possible reasons for looking at budget numbers or for setting budget targets. One has to do with aggregate demand, whether the public sector actions lead to a net increase or decrease in absorption. The other has to do with financial markets, whether financing public sector deficits in some particular money-debt mix adversely affects interest rates.

In either case, any budgetary adjustment for inflation assumes an exactly offsetting increase in private sector saving. A statement that the government deficit is no source of concern because it merely reflects inflationary amortization of liabilities may distort the impact on aggregate demand, the current account, and financial markets. Without a matching increase in private saving, a larger budget deficit, because of increased inflation, still means higher aggregate demand, a larger current account deficit, and an excess flow supply of government financial assets. But unless the change in inflation is completely neutral there can be no presumption that rises in private sector saving will match increases in budget deficits, one for one. Shifts in portfolio composition in response to inflation and inflation taxes suggest that the compensation will be incomplete. Failing an exact matching there is no way around a more detailed planning of the public sector in terms of taxes, real spending, capital transfers, and debt service.

The correction for inflation is meant to help assess the sustainability of a current fiscal stance. If fiscal policies, correctly measured, imply *trend* increases in the real stock of government liabilities relative to income (or relative to the tax base or capital), then policy is on a bad track. This interpretation suggests that we want to use the inflation correction as an improvement on our trend-deficit measure. It also means that a careful distinction should be made between once-and-for-all changes in the real value of government liabilities and the trend-growth rate. Government liabilities are affected by nonrecurrent transactions and by sharp transitory inflation that is not matched by changes in interest rates.

It is hard to see why Bacha believes that the domestic currency-denominated public sector borrowing requirement, unadjusted for inflation, serves the IMF for "ill-hidden ideological purposes." On the contrary, the procedure is strongly geared to ensuring external performance, almost irrespective of the macroeconomic performance of the economy. As Bacha notes, the public sector ceilings are not a particularly effective tool for controlling inflation. The public sector budget does, however, figure in the current account identity that links the real sectoral balances:

(2) Current account deficit = Budget deficit (unadjusted) + $(I-S)$

where $I-S$ denotes private sector investment *less* saving. If the target were set in terms of the "true deficit" $\Delta[(B+EB^*)/P]$, changes in the real exchange rate or the rate of inflation would affect the current account. Since IMF programs are concerned with external adjustment (why else would anyone go to the IMF?) it seems plausible that policy instruments (the budget) would be linked as tightly as possible to policy objectives or constraints (the external balance).

There is, though, some rationale to Bacha's argument, as follows. Once the government deficit is set in real terms, a realistic inflation forecast becomes essential to set overall performance criteria for the raw deficit. Otherwise the program either has no chance of being implemented—the Brazilian case—or, if implemented, can devastate the economy. Thus, inflation forecasts are essential for moving from real targets to nominal performance criteria, but it is highly implausible that the IMF would deliberately bias the inflation forecast down. The issue, then, is not the treatment of changes in the real value of public sector liabilities but rather the realistic forecasting of inflation.

Bacha's second criticism takes the IMF to task for its deflationary bias. The current account, he argues, is being regarded from the perspective of saving and investment, ignoring the special roles of export constraints and credit limitations. Bacha's point is illustrated in an IMF commentary on the Brazilian program that contains the full cliché[3]:

> Thus the economic program calls for a significant reduction in domestic spending and a subsequent strengthening of domestic savings, in particular by the public sector. To limit the negative effects on the standard of living, the authorities intend to raise economic efficiency through liberalization of the economy early in the program.

It is an accounting truth that the current account can improve only if domestic saving (public and private combined) increases or investment declines, or both. But that does not mean that a strategy of raising saving pursued through budget cutting will promote a *high employment* current account improvement. Such a long-run adjustment requires price flexibility and a reallocation of resources that will occur neither spontaneously nor fast, as the Chilean case has so dramatically demonstrated.

This implies that, along with budget cutting, changes are needed in real exchange rates or export subsidies that actively promote employment of the resources "saved" in the public sector. That used to be standard IMF policy, well in line with the Meade-Swan-Johnson policy prescription of expenditure-reducing and expenditure-switching measures to correct deficits with a maximum use of resources. Unfortunately, the IMF failed to insist on this in the original program. One hopes this does not represent a change in the more basic IMF conception of stabilization policy, as some of the new language about liberalization and other supply-side fads might suggest.

But Bacha is surely not right in arguing that export constraints make the current account identity in any way a defective conceptual framework. Export constraints simply mean two things: first that adjustment will be more costly; second, that great attention must be paid to achieving domestic and international cost competitiveness. That means, when there are export constraints, an aggressive beggar-my-neighbor policy has to be pursued through domestic and international real depreciation and possibly through regional, discriminatory arrangements as well.

As a world system, beggar-my-neighbor is, of course, exceptionally poor policy. But such systemic concerns are a matter for advanced countries, and for developing countries as a group. For individual developing countries, aggressive real depreciation is the best policy advice.

---

[3] *IMF Survey* (March 21, 1983), p. 93.

True, it cuts real wages of persons still employed, but because employment is the main determinant of the welfare of the poor, it remains the best policy advice.

Brazil has undertaken some real depreciation. I am not persuaded that the real depreciation undertaken is anywhere near the right size to achieve a high-employment improvement in the external balance, because a considerable number of competitor countries are doing precisely the same thing and domestic public sector price corrections imply major increases in nonwage costs relative to the rest of the world. In other words, the public sector deficit provided implicit export subsidies (energy prices, for example) that now have to be compensated by open, real depreciation.

Bacha calls for incomes policy as an alternative to the present-style stand-by program. He does not give much content to what such an incomes policy-oriented program might look like. I would think its key feature would be an emphasis on low real rates of interest to stop the redistribution of income from operating firms to bondholders that is now proving destructive to real activity. Second, the program should include a wage, exchange rate, and public sector pricing policy that ensures a sustained, significant real depreciation. Last, the program must definitely include fiscal reform that increases revenues and, possibly, reduces the extent of real debt service. In many ways, reenacting the policies of 1964 would be a highly desirable policy package. Progressive economists have poo-poohed those policies for years, but it is clear now that the 1964 package was one of the more successful stabilization programs both in respect to the social costs and to longer term viability.

OTHER ISSUES

I conclude my remarks with three points meant to stimulate discussion. First, economic theory provides very little guidance, as yet, to the question of a strategy for optimal external borrowing and growth. In a world where both real interest rates and real export earnings are stochastic and correlated, what is the optimal rule? Surely the answer will not be to borrow short-term for long-term projects, expecting that an adverse run will never occur. The Brazilian 1979-81 experience suggests, ex post, the costs can be extreme, even if they eventuate only once every fifty years. Institutionally, as a side aspect of this issue, there should be an international provision that helps debtor countries during episodes of high real interest rates just as there are IMF facilities for periods of low real commodity prices. Such a "real interest facility" is important in order to separate problems of structural imbalance from those of temporary disturbances.

My second point concerns the Brazilian recipe for growth. Over the last fifteen years, growth has benefited from a large, continuing public sector investment program. Under any of the programs now being considered, investment will be sharply reduced and so will be the public sector presence which has operated as an automatic stabilizer. It stands to reason that over the next ten (not just two or three) years, growth performance will dramatically deteriorate and social progress with it.

My third point concerns direct foreign investment. Latin America, and Brazil more particularly, has celebrated a festival of nationalism in which extravagant foreign borrowing has replaced what should have been, to a much larger extent, equity financing. The issue here is not the size of the current account deficit but its financing. The government has guaranteed an external dollar debt that it is in a poor position to assure either politically or economically. It has thereby exposed itself unnecessarily by "refusing to sell the country." Just as indexed bonds are a vengeance when real tax revenues are low, so too external debt proves a problem in adverse conditions. If more of the current account had been financed by direct foreign investment and less by debt, the international sharing of adverse events would involve much less extreme variations in domestic welfare. Instead of a debt crisis arising from increased real interest payments and reduced export earnings, remittances of dividends would simply have been reduced.

3 The Exchange Crisis and the Adjustment Program in Mexico

Ariel Buira

It is a singular distinction and a pleasure for me to appear before such a knowledgeable audience to discuss recent developments in the Mexican economy and prospects for our adjustment program.

The Mexican economy grew rapidly between 1978 and 1981, with aggregate demand continuously stimulated by a high level of public spending. With the opportunities afforded by the oil sector, together with the availability of domestic and foreign credit, investment expanded at an unprecedented rate as of 1978. As the magnitude of the oil fields became known both at home and abroad, and the enormous public investments in the field of energy had their effect on aggregate demand, access of Mexico's public agencies and private firms to international financial markets was greatly enhanced.

As time went by, rigidities and bottlenecks became increasingly evident, feeding the inflationary process. Consumer prices rose by 16 percent in 1978, 20 percent in 1979, and almost 30 percent in 1980 and 1981.

In an attempt to moderate inflation, increases of prices and tariffs of goods and services provided by the public sector were postponed. A significant portion of the oil revenue was transferred to the public through subsidies, thus postponing an adjustment in the price level. These policies resulted in the medium term in a worsening of the structural dis-

---

Dr. Buira is deputy director, Banco de Mexico.

equilibrium of public finances, which eventually had very serious adverse effects.

As the inflation differential between Mexico and the United States increased, the peso became overvalued. Continued overspending by the public sector plus the overvaluation of the peso pushed imports to record levels and were also fundamental factors in the large purchases of foreign assets (real estate and financial assets) by Mexicans. Oil wealth lent support to the notion held by many businessmen that a permanent overvaluation of the peso was feasible and would allow them to finance investments and the acquisition of equity by means of foreign credits, at a cost equal to the interest rate on foreign loans, which was considerably lower than that prevailing in Mexico.

Because of the sharp increase in oil prices between 1979 and 1980, and also due to the increased production of crude oil, revenues from oil exports increased from $3.8 billion to $9.4 billion. Prices of other important exports, such as coffee, silver, and cotton, also rose. This resulted in a sharp improvement in the country's terms of trade in both 1979 and 1980.

In an attempt to speed up development in a decisive manner, create employment, increase welfare, and improve income distribution, Mexico spent its oil revenue and resorted to additional external financing. It should be acknowledged that very important progress was achieved on all these fronts. Output and employment registered high rates of growth in the period 1978–81. Real GDP increased at more than 8 percent a year and the ratio of gross domestic investment to GDP rose to around 28 percent, some 5 to 6 percentage points higher than in 1977. This strong expansion of investment helped bring about a substantial increase in employment; gains in employment averaged more than 5 percent a year, well in excess of the growth rate of the labor force.

However, the resulting demand pressures together with an increasingly overvalued exchange rate and the greater openness of the economy resulted in growing external imbalances.

Industrial nations reacted to the 1979–80 price hikes and to inflationary pressures by adopting restrictive financial policies and seeking to protect employment through protectionist measures. As a result, worldwide economic activity declined in 1980; the depression continued through 1981 and 1982. This in turn was reflected by a reduction in the volume of international trade. The effect of the international economic recession on Mexico's exports was significant, particularly on oil sales. As the price of oil started to fall during the first half of 1981, marketing problems emerged which resulted in a substantial decrease in foreign exchange earnings.

Income from other major exports was also seriously affected. The price of silver, for example, which had reached almost $40 an ounce in early 1980, dropped to $8.20 by the end of 1981. Tourism was also affected by the overvaluation of the peso and the worldwide economic recession.

Moreover, the anti-inflationary strategy adopted by major industrial countries led to increases in interest rates, which reached historically high levels in both nominal and real terms. As a result, foreign debt-service payments soared.

These adverse developments had a major impact on the Mexican balance of payments, which in 1981 recorded a current account deficit of $12.5 billion. In fact, the actual deficit may have been larger, given the size of the entry for errors and omissions (−$8.3 billion). In response, an adjustment program was adopted in mid-1981, consisting of a 4 percent reduction in government expenditures, the introduction of import licences, and increases in the prices of gasoline and other price controlled goods.

However, these adjustment measures proved to be late and insufficient. They were not able to reduce significantly the size of the domestic and external disequilibria. In fact, the financial deficit of the public sector reached a record level of 14.6 percent of GDP in 1981. The continuing deterioration of the balance of payments created the expectation that the gradual depreciation of the exchange rate would be insufficient to correct the imbalances on current account. As a result, savings were increasingly channeled toward dollar-denominated deposits, and capital flight reached unprecedented levels. During the second half of 1981, the government decided to offset declining foreign exchange revenues through active external borrowing which, for the most part, was contracted at short-term maturities.

At the start of 1982, the exchange rate continued to be subject to strong pressures. The outlook was grim as international oil markets continued to weaken, interest rates remained at extremely high levels, and the United States (Mexico's principal trade partner) was in the midst of a protracted recession. In February, as capital flight intensified, the policy of a gradual depreciation of the exchange rate was abandoned. On February 18, the peso was allowed to float reaching a level of 45 pesos to the dollar—that is a 67 percent depreciation.

Immediately after the devaluation, a new set of economic policy measures was announced. Even though external factors had contributed to the crisis, the need to make major adjustments in public finances in order to reduce the public deficit was explicitly acknowledged.

Among the most important measures was a 3 percent reduction in the federal budget. Price controls were tightened, while tariffs for some 1,500 items, mainly raw materials and capital goods, were reduced. At the same time, more flexible interest and exchange rate policies were adopted in an attempt to avoid a new overvaluation of the peso.

However, before the effects of these measures could be felt, a large wage adjustment was granted in March, which justifiably had very unfavorable repercussions on public expectations. Capital flight resumed although a trade surplus was attained for the first time in several years.

As confidence dwindled, public and private enterprises had increasing difficulties in obtaining fresh funds and/or rescheduling credit lines. Diminished external credit, coupled with increased capital flight and short-term debt payments, caused a considerable reduction in the international reserves of the country.

On August 5, in the face of a rapidly eroding international reserve position, new exchange measures were put into effect in an attempt to prevent capital flight and to reduce the inflationary impact of exchange rate adjustments. A two-tier exchange system was established with a preferential rate for debt service and high priority imports, and a general rate to be determined on the free market for all other transactions.

On August 13, in order to eliminate the risk of massive transfers of foreign currency abroad, which would have exhausted existing reserves, dollar denominated accounts in Mexican banks, the so-called "Mex-dollars" amounting to approximately $12 billion, were made payable only in pesos.

On the same date, the foreign exchange market was temporarily closed. After a six-day bank holiday, foreign currency operations resumed with a 69.5 exchange rate for Mex-dollars, and a free market rate which fluctuated between 100 and 120 pesos per dollar.

On August 20 a 90-day extension of public external debt payments on principal was obtained while a debt restructuring proposal was under preparation and negotiations with the International Monetary Fund commenced.

On September 1, for the first time in Mexico's history, comprehensive exchange controls were established, and the nationalization of commercial banks was decreed.

Immediately after the implementation of exchange controls, a peso market developed in several US border towns. A large proportion of Mexico's foreign currency receipts were channeled through this market, particularly proceeds from private merchandise exports, tourism and requirements for local expenditures of the in-bond (offshore assembly) industries. Only a small proportion of the foreign currency revenues was channeled through the banking system. As a result, capital flight continued and the shortage of foreign exchange became acute.

THE ECONOMIC ADJUSTMENT PROGRAM, 1983–85

The new administration, which took office on December 1, established an adjustment program geared to the reordering of the economy ("Programa Imediato de Reordenación Económica"). The program was designed to reduce inflation and strengthen the balance of payments, in order to prepare for the resumption of sustained growth of output and employment. Its fundamental elements are the improvement of public finances and an increase in domestic savings. As a result of these policies, the rate of inflation should decline substantially in 1983 and more gradually over the program period. When the program is completed, the underlying rate of inflation should be under reasonable control. It was recognized that an unavoidable result would be negligible growth of real GDP in 1983, but a resumption of growth was planned in 1984 and 1985, to 3 percent and 6 percent, respectively.

The reduction of the public sector deficit was recognized as the key factor in the control of domestic demand, strengthening of the external position, and so limiting the need for external financing. The planned improvement of public finances involves a reduction of the public sector deficit—from the equivalent of 16.5 percent in 1982 to 8.5 percent of GDP in 1983, to 5.5 percent in 1984, and to 3.5 percent in 1985—which should allow the restoration of public sector savings. The cutback in the public sector deficit should also make it possible to increase the volume of credit to the private sector.

The current account deficit of the balance of payments was expected to decline from $13 billion in 1981 to $3 billion in 1983. The improvement in the current account would reflect the expected achievement of considerable surpluses in the balance of goods and nonfactor services, mostly as a result of an increasing trade surplus. Nonoil exports should rise in response to the expected economic recovery abroad and the improved competitiveness of the domestic economy arising from a flexible exchange rate policy. The share of total imports in aggregate supply should decline, particularly during the first part of the adjustment period. These trends should permit a gradual recovery of net international reserves and a more efficient allocation of available resources.

Monetary policy should be consistent with the anti-inflationary and balance of payments aims of the program. Credit policy will allocate an increasing share of domestic financial savings to the private sector, with limits placed on credit to the public sector. Interest rate policy will be managed flexibly; to promote saving, attractive rates will be offered in relation to expected inflation.

External debt, as a proportion of GDP, should decline both during and beyond the program period. The program includes limits on net foreign borrowing by the public sector: the rate of increase in external public debt decreases significantly over the program period.

The restructuring of most amortization due in 1983 and 1984, as well as that postponed during the period August–December 1982 (around $20 billion), including the refinancing on a medium-term basis of all short-term obligations outstanding ($9.5 billion), has resulted in a significant improvement in the maturity structure of the external public debt. Special mechanisms have been established for the settlement of arrears on interest payments due by private borrowers to foreign commercial banks and for the restructuring of private debt.

Exchange rate policy will be conducted flexibly in order to maintain the competitiveness of the economy and to help reconstitute international reserves. Major export promotion efforts will be implemented, and as the reserve position permits the protective system will be revised with a view to rationalizing the structure of protection and reducing the level of effective protection to improve resource allocation.

Incomes policy is another key element of the program. Wage policy will be oriented to the achievement of medium-term employment objectives and will be consistent with a declining rate of inflation. Price controls will be kept under review in order to avoid discouraging production and employment while assuring that profit margins are kept within reasonable limits.

Since an equitable distribution of the costs of adjustment among the population is a basic aim of the government, subsidies will be used selectively to protect the living standards of the lower income groups. In addition emergency employment programs will be implemented in critical rural and urban areas during 1983 through selective budget expenditure.

A PROGRESS REPORT

The first quarter of 1983 has been particularly difficult for the Mexican economy: the costs of adjustment have become apparent, while positive results largely still remain to be seen.

Economic activity contracted sharply in the first quarter, reflecting a significant decline in aggregate demand, while inflationary pressures remained at high (albeit declining) levels. Manufacturing output declined by some 11 percent to 12 percent below the levels of a year ago, a decline that was particularly marked in the production of capital goods, automobiles, and durable consumer goods. Construction activity also fell sharply. As a result, employment diminished. The number of employed workers covered by the Social Security Institute declined some 4 percent in relation to the levels of the first quarter of 1982. In fact, the decline in employment is probably larger since the construction industry, one of those showing a particularly large fall, is one in which the use of casual labor, usually not covered by Social Security, is the rule rather than the exception.

Public finances recorded a significant improvement despite the shortfall in revenues from income and value-added taxes due to the decline in the level of economic activity and the exchange losses suffered by many firms. The overall public sector deficit declined by 23 percent below the level of the first quarter of 1982, in nominal terms. Government revenues rose by 113 percent and government expenditures by 97 percent. Revenues of public enterprises increased by 150 percent while their expenditures, including investment, increased by 48 percent.

The restoration of interest rates to realistic levels in December stimulated a recovery of bank deposits which was apparent during the first quarter of 1983. However, demand for credit has been low, reflecting the low levels of production and investment and the liquid position of many firms that have not been able to make external debt payments due to the shortage of foreign exchange.

Money supply has shown a declining trend, passing from an annual growth rate of 60 percent in January, to 57 percent in February, and 40 percent in March. These rates of monetary expansion are substantially below those of prices and suggest a rapid reduction in the liquidity of the economy.

During the first four months of 1983, consumer prices increased by 30 percent, with inflation showing a clear downward trend in January–

March and a jump in April due to increases in gasoline and other administered prices.

Despite the decline in oil prices, the external sector strengthened considerably in response to the exchange rate adjustment and the decline in activity. The balance of trade for the first quarter recorded a surplus of some \$3.4 billion, largely as a result of a decline in imports to \$1.5 billion, less than one-third their level a year earlier. Exports of oil increased some \$600 million, an increase that was partially offset by a decline in other exports of goods. In addition, tourism and border trade recorded a \$380 million surplus during the quarter.

The exchange market has stabilized despite the delays in the first drawings under the \$5 billion commercial bank facility and the decline in the oil price with the differential between the controlled and the free market rate narrowing considerably. Rapid progress was also made in restructuring the public external debt and the establishment of mechanisms for restructuring the private sector debt, and in the normalization of trade and payments.

ISSUES FOR DISCUSSION

Since stabilization programs are more an art than a science there are, as in other cases, a number of uncertainties and questions. The questions that arise most frequently are two:

- Is the program too strict to be consistent with social and political stability?
- Does this type of program provide the best solution to the problems of economies that have to make major structural adjustments?

Since we have seen that excess demand, arising largely from fiscal deficits, played a major role in the imbalances that developed in the Mexican economy, the reduction of these imbalances necessarily played a large role in the adjustment program. Therefore the question relates more to the size of the adjustment than to the direction of policy. To an important degree the fiscal target for 1983 (the large reduction in the public sector deficit) was the outcome of an exogenous factor, the availability of external finance. After the virtual closing of the international financial markets to Mexico in 1982, access to \$5 billion net borrowing in 1983 appeared extremely unlikely. In fact, this sum could only be contracted after some delay, with the personal involvement of the IMF managing director and the support of the monetary authorities of the major industrial countries. The sum of the financial resources available appears adequate to meet the demand for external payments, including debt service after the restructuring of public external debt, at the level of economic activity foreseen.

The political issue is to persuade the public of the need for austerity. The task is to carry through this reduction in the standards of living of the various sectors of the population in a manner that is equitable and socially acceptable. The Mexican population has enjoyed a sustained increase in living standards for over a generation, with a rapid improvement in recent years. The process of reducing actual levels of consumption and adjusting expectations about standards of living is painful.

The adjustment program agreeing with the IMF assumed no growth in real GDP in 1983. However, since income and employment increased rapidly in the preceding years, this setback, though unfortunate, could be regarded as inevitable.

The target for reducing inflation is necessarily ambitious and there has been progress in reducing inflation from rates in excess of 10 percent a month to monthly rates of around 5 percent. On the basis of current policies, we expect a further reduction in the coming months. To conclude, Mexico is engaged in an ambitious economic program designed to strengthen the external sector, reduce dependence on external financing, and lower inflation. The full benefits of the program will not be felt for some time, but progress so far has been satisfactory and prospects for success are favorable.

Since in most cases the severity of an adjustment program can be diminished only by additional external finance, it is a matter of judgment whether existing international arrangements provide assurance of a sufficient volume of resources to support the adjustment process in an orderly manner. It should be noted that a shortage of liquidity reduces the possibilities of success of a program and thereby raises the risk attached to the financial assets of the creditors.

A related issue concerns the cumulative impact of a number of severe adjustment programs (leading to declining GDP and imports in major developing and developed countries) on world trade and a weak economic recovery. Note that Mexico alone, the third largest US trading partner in 1981, reduced its total imports of goods and services by some $10 billion in 1982 and these may decline further in 1983.

The developing countries account for over 25 percent of all exports from the Organization for Economic Cooperation and Development (OECD) countries, 38 percent of US exports, and 45 percent of Japanese exports. An effort by these countries to improve their payments positions based to a great extent on the reduction of imports, at least in 1983, will have a substantial impact on the export earnings of industrial countries.

Let us now consider a further issue: whether the adjustment programs of other Latin American countries are the most appropriate manner to promote rapid structural adjustment of these economies.

While the structural nature of the adjustment required by many developing countries today calls for large amounts of medium-term finance, the trend is for reduced flows, shorter maturities, and higher spreads as a way of limiting the risks associated with international lending.

The emergence of problems in the international capital markets and the increased importance of structural problems suggest the need for international organizations to stand ready to finance a larger part of the countries' payments imbalances during the adjustment process. For this larger role the Fund would require substantially greater resources than were provided recently by the Interim Committee under the Eighth Quota Review. This is necessary to allow the Fund to play a larger role as a financial intermediary and to meet the greater demands on its resources in the difficult conditions of the current decade.

Additional resources for the Fund and the World Bank are essential if they are to be in a position to assist countries in the correction of structural imbalances. Structural adjustments will require, in addition to demand management policies, substantial investment programs to expand output in key sectors; these programs should be encouraged and supported to the greatest extent, even if they may result in a weaker trade account in the short run, since in the medium term they will lead to a stronger external and budgetary position. Structural adjustment programs would permit the achievement of a more viable external position and higher rates of growth both during the life of the adjustment program and in the longer run, with consequent benefits for the countries concerned and for the international economy.

Discussion

William R. Cline

Ariel Buira has provided an excellent review of the problems of economic adjustment facing Mexico. Broadly his evaluation is optimistic. Without necessarily disputing the main thrust of his assessment, I would like to highlight some of the potential costs and risks involved in the adjustment program.

Fundamentally the most important question is how costly it will be in terms of growth to meet the objectives of the adjustment program. Mexico's budget deficit is to be cut from 16½ percent of GDP in 1982 to 8½ percent in 1983 and lower thereafter. It is striking that in the three papers for this conference there is sharp disagreement on the implications of such austerity for economic growth. For Brazil, Edmar L. Bacha suggests that the targeted budget cutback by a somewhat smaller relative magnitude could reduce GDP by 15 percent; but the authors of the Mexico and Argentina studies place only limited emphasis on possible recessionary effects of considerably larger budget cutbacks.

One senses a lack of firm theoretical guidelines here. Under (Keynesian) textbook macroeconomics, if it could be argued that the economy is at overfull employment, budgetary restraint would merely reduce inflation, not real output. But there is little reason to believe that these economies are at full employment of resources, and surely the cuts in aggregate demand will have at least a temporary impact on real growth. The saving grace—in the classic IMF stabilization model—is the expansionary stimulus to exports from devaluation. Even ignoring the possible critique of inelastic export response, in Mexico's case the prospective rise in exports seems likely to be only about 1.7 percent of GDP in 1983—far below the recessionary reduction in aggregate demand

---

Dr. Cline is a senior fellow at the Institute for International Economics.

from contraction in the budget deficit. Thus, even without considering multiplier effects, the net decline in aggregate demand (on the order of 6 percent of GDP) seems likely to pose a problem of serious recession.

The external sector target also has implications for growth. It must be kept in mind that Mexico already had a sharp decline of imports in 1982, from $24 billion in 1981 to only $14 billion. That cutback came at the expense of growth, which fell from 8 percent to zero, as imported inputs for industry became scarce. The reduction in imports reflected sheer unavailability of foreign exchange, raising the question of whether much further reduction can be expected in 1983 on a sustainable basis despite the sharp real devaluation. The external target itself has undergone a curious evolution. It began as a 1983 current account deficit of $3.4 billion—the premise of the IMF and private bank package. Then, even after the loss of $1.4 billion for 1983 as the consequence of a cut in the price of oil by $3 per barrel, the official projection actually improved to a small current account surplus ($300 million) for the year. The official argument was that initial overstatement of 1983 interest payments, and a much slower import rate than expected, meant the year's deficit would be even smaller than originally expected despite weaker oil prices. Buira's paper reports, indeed, that first-quarter imports were only $1.5 billion—an annual rate that, at only 42 percent of the full-year 1982 level, surely cannot be kept as low through the rest of the year.

As in the case of the domestic budget target, however, Mexico seems likely to have to pay a high price in growth if a very low foreign deficit is to be met. Mexico can either have a current account balance near zero or it can have zero growth (as officials hoped)—it cannot have both. A zero current account balance seems much more likely to require growth on the order of −5 percent to −6 percent. And even the original target ($3.4 billion deficit) seems more consistent with, perhaps, −3 percent growth than with the zero-growth target. In sum, achievement of both the internal and external targets run the risk of a severe recession. Correspondingly, if the loss in growth is to be minimized, the external (and perhaps internal budgetary) target is likely not to be met. For this reason one cannot discount the possibility that Mexico will need to appeal to international private and official creditors for an additional $2 billion to $3 billion in support even in 1983, despite the large trade surplus in the first quarter.

Capital flight is an area of possible concern. Reaching approximately $8 billion in 1981 and again in 1982, it was clearly responsible for much of Mexico's financial problem. It is not clear how firmly the channels for capital flight have been sealed. The government appears to be supporting the free market rate of 150 pesos per dollar, and potentially this practice could lead to capital flight once again.

Domestic inflation is another area of concern. If the monthly rate of inflation holds at the 5 percent trend (after the April surge), inflation would again be 100 percent for the year, far above target.

The greatest vulnerability of the program, however, stems from the severe decline in real incomes it implies and the corresponding potential for political unacceptability. The wage increase of 25 percent in January will either have to be supplemented by much larger increases than the 12½ percent programmed for July, or real wages will fall precipitously. It must be kept in mind that Mexico does not have indexation, and 100 percent inflation must involve much more random human sacrifice than a similar rate in Brazil. Moreover, the prospect of real income losses is heightened by the likelihood of severe recession, perhaps 4 percent to 5 percent decline in GNP, that may be required to keep imports sufficiently low to meet the balance of payments (current account) target. Indeed, the ultimate unknown in the Mexican and other major adjustment programs is where the breaking point occurs in domestic political tolerance.

There are also economic vulnerabilities. The greatest—although not necessarily the most likely—is a collapse in the price of oil. With oil at $20 to $22 per barrel, Mexico's external deficit could rise to $10 billion yearly. Even continued stagnation at $29 per barrel will mean pressure on external accounts as import prices rise. Another vulnerability is a possible breakdown of the process of involuntary lending. The banks must continue lending to Mexico, and it remains to be seen whether the successful mobilization of new lending for 1983 can be repeated in 1984 and 1985. The difficulty of encouraging smaller banks to increase their exposure is well known.

In sum, the remarkable feat of Mexico's seeming adherence to a difficult external sector target, despite a drop in the price of oil, warrants only two cheers at the present time, until the potential growth costs and political strain are demonstrated to be within tolerable bounds. Nonetheless, the international financial community must be gratified by the external sector progress to date. Hopefully, international economic recovery will mitigate these costs and stresses over the next five years. However, if global recession persists, there will be a rather high probability of collapse in the adjustment programs of Mexico and other major debtors, and of orderly adherence even to their rescheduled debt obligations.